NATIVE AMERICAN BEAD WEAVING

NATIVE AMERICAN BEAD WEAVING

LYNNE GARNER

GUILD OF MASTER CRAFTSMAN PUBLICATIONS

First published 2003 by
Guild of Master Craftsman Publications Ltd
166 High Street, Lewes
East Sussex, BN7 1XU

Reprinted 2004

Photographic Credits:
Step-by-step photographs supplied by Lynne Garner
Finished projects photographed by Anthony Bailey,
GMC Publications Photographic Studio.
Saffron Walden Museum: p. 2
Topham Picturepoint: p. 4
Royal Geographic Society: p. 3
Hugh Harrop (www.hughharrop.com): p. 94

Illustrations by Simon Rodway

ISBN 1 86108 281 9

British Cataloguing in Publication Data
A catalogue record of this book is available from the British Library.

Designed by Phil and Traci Morash, Fineline Studios
Typeface: Foundry Sans

Colour origination by Viscan Graphics Pte Ltd (Singapore)
Printed and bound by Kyodo Printing (Singapore)

DEDICATION

To a mum who is always trying to discover new craft
'toys' for me, thanks.

A thank you also to the following people, for their
help and support during the research and writing
of this book:

Jon, my fiancé, and my family and friends for their
continued support and understanding. Thanks, Jon,
for putting up with me in 'week ten' when I sat in front
of the television, yet again with a lap full of loom,
beads and design sheets.

Uncle Albert for making me my wonderful
jointed loom.

The staff of Saffron Walden Museum for their help
and for allowing me the privilege of handling and
photographing some of their wonderful Native
American artefacts.

Fred Aldous for the supply of materials, both beads
and large loom.

Craft Creations for the supply of card and peel 'n'
sticks, and The Rocking Rabbit Trading Co.

CONTENTS

THE PROJECTS

INTRODUCTION

Like many people, I first encountered bead weaving when I received a gift of a basic weaving kit containing a loom, beads, thread and some limited instructions.

Once I had completed my first piece of weaving, I had to decide what to do with it, and so began my search for crafting items that I could decorate with my newly found bead-weaving skills. During this search I became truly engrossed in this wonderful craft.

Bead weaving is both fun and easy and I hope this book will inspire you to bead all manner of items for yourself, your family, friends and for your home. Have fun – and you may even create a family heirloom along the way.

A Brief History

Beads are steeped in history, as are their many uses and the forms of art and craft that are associated with them. It is believed that the simplest and earliest form of bead weaving was hand held, using techniques similar to that of braiding. This first form was known as 'finger weaving'. Unlike the loom-weaving method that will be used in this book (known as single-strand weaving, where a single weft thread is taken under and over the warp threads) finger weaving did not have a separate warp and weft thread, instead two weft threads were used. The left weft thread was passed through the bead one way and the right weft thread was passed through the bead in the opposite direction. On the next row the threads were taken back through the beads the other way.

Without the written word, or many surviving artefacts, it is difficult to find the true roots of bead weaving. Some early examples of looms do exist, however, and one of the earliest is known as the bow loom. This was constructed using a

Original Native American bead weaving on two pouches

flexible stick with heddles (made of birch bark or bone) to separate the warp threads at either end. The thread itself was made from a variety of materials including hide thong, twisted animal sinew – still used today by some African craftspeople who make jewellery from ostrich eggshell – and cord made from a variety of plants (dogbane stalks, basswood bark and cedar bark were just some of the most commonly used).

Some of the methods that were employed were very similar in style to those used to weave baskets. There were, however, limitations to the bow loom and experiments were made with other forms of loom. One, which is the basis for the loom we use today, was a simple rectangular box loom. This was constructed from four pieces of wood, which were simply fastened together at each corner.

As with the loom, many details of the development of beads are lost in the mists of time, but it is known that a large number of materials were used in the making of beads, the earliest being made from natural materials. Shells were a favourite raw material and beads created from shell found in Lindenmeier, Colorado, USA are believed to be 11,500 years old. These beads were found 1,300km (800 miles) as the bird flies from the nearest source, so they had travelled a great distance via trade – and perhaps as gifts – to reach their final resting place, which demonstrates their importance to the indigenous people of America.

Bead weaving adorned many items, including belts, dresses, headbands and footwear, and different tribes favoured different forms of decoration – for example, some preferred geometric designs while others specialized in flowers or depictions of animals – and so today experts working in this field are able to tell which tribe produced which artefact. Different tribes not only favoured different motifs but also different

Native American woman with bead necklace

ways of attaching their beads to the items they were making. For example the Sioux seldom used floral designs, as they used a stitch called 'lazy stitch' to attach their beads, which restricted them to patterns and blocks of colour.

The wampum is perhaps the best-known Native American bead. This is a small, rounded, pierced disc or oval cut from a freshwater mussel, and examples exist which date from the 1600s or before. The word 'wampum' is from the Narragansett word which translates as 'white shell beads'. Wampum beads were crafted in two colours, white and purple. The white beads came from the whelk/busycon shell and purple-black

Native American beaded caps

The Crow tribe also prized beads and would use them for trading with the newly arrived Europeans. They, however, sought the highly prized glass pony beads, which were brought from Italy by the French traders. They were nicknamed 'pony beads' after the method of their arrival, via the beast of burden, the pony. These pony beads came in limited colours, mainly blue, white, black and red and, at 3mm (⅛in) across, were both larger than the beads we use for bead weaving today and slightly irregular in shape. As they arrived ready-to-use, the laborious task of making them was avoided, and the Native Americans quickly adopted the pony beads. The Crow were so fond of pony beads that they would trade a horse for 100 beads, and the horse was an important survival tool, which they used both for hunting and travel.

The seed beads that we associate and use in bead weaving today were not introduced to the Native Americans until the 1850s. These small glass beads were imported from Czechoslovakia and replaced the home-made beads which they had produced for their own use. So, although an age-old craft, bead weaving has changed and grown over the centuries to the form we recognize and practise today. I am sure it will continue to adapt and grow and stay just as fresh and exciting as it has been for the many generations of crafters who beaded before us.

beads from the growth rings of the quahog/merinaria shell. Prior to the arrival of the Europeans the beads were large with big holes, but when metal awls were introduced the size of the bead decreased as the size of the hole was reduced.

When trading first took place between the Europeans and the Native Americans the lack of metal coinage was a problem and, to overcome this, the beads became the formal currency. A fathom (183cm/6ft) of strung white wampum beads was worth 10 shillings, and worth 20 shillings if the beads were purple. A fathom, which held between 240 to 360 beads, depending upon their size, became known as Wampumpeage or Peage and was a signifier of monetary value. This use of wampum as money, even among the Europeans, continued until the American Revolution began in 1775.

BEAD WEAVING BASICS

Basic bead weaving is fun and addictive. Looms come in a variety of shapes and sizes, and prices are inexpensive compared to items for some other crafts. Once you have mastered bead weaving, all you need to replenish is the beads and the thread and both can be found at a reasonable price. It is your imagination and design skills that are put to the test with this craft, not the depth of your purse or wallet.

BASIC TERMS

BEADING NEEDLE

This needle is made specifically for beading, rather than bead weaving. It has a smaller eye than normal, so it will pass through the hole in the bead.

BEADING THREAD

This is stronger than normal sewing thread and is usually lightly coated, so that the fibres of the thread do not catch on the bead as it passes through.

COLUMN

The term used for the beads that follow the direction of the warp threads.

HEDDLE

This part of the loom is used to space the warp threads equally across it.

LAZY STITCH

A long straight stitch, used for creating blocks of shapes.

ROW (OF BEADS)

This is the term used for the beads that follow the direction of the weft threads.

WARP

Warp threads are those that run the full length of the loom, i.e. from top to bottom. They are fastened securely to the rollers at either end of the loom and the beads sit between them.

WEFT

Weft threads run from left to right, across the warp threads. The beads are threaded onto these threads during the weaving process and the thread passes through the beads twice, under the warp thread the first time, then over it the second time, when the thread is taken back.

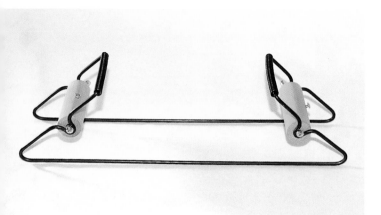

Simple metal frame loom

Simple wooden frame loom

MATERIALS AND EQUIPMENT

BASIC MATERIALS AND EQUIPMENT YOU WILL NEED:

- Thread to match beads being used
- Bead loom
- Small scissors for cutting threads
- Beading needle (length to suit project)

Certain additional items will be needed for each project, and these will be specified in the respective Materials lists. They will include jewellery findings, such as clasps, crimp rings, necklet ends and ear wires (available in a variety of styles, including 'kidney' or 'shepherd's crook'), which can be obtained from many bead or jewellery suppliers.

As well as the jewellery findings, you will require round-nose pliers and/or bull-nose pliers.

BEAD LOOM

The bead-weaving loom comes in a variety of guises and sizes, and ranges from a simple metal frame to the more complicated, adjustable split loom. There are also small tubular looms, ideal – but not essential – for creating rings (the ring projects included here were made on a standard

Loom for creating bracelets

Split adjustable loom

Tubular loom for ring weaving

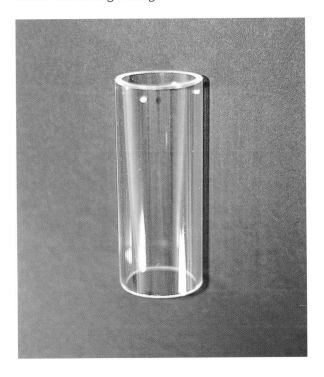

loom). All function in the same sort of way, allowing you to anchor a number of threads, held at the correct tension, while you weave. The simple wooden or metal frame loom, available boxed and with full instructions, is probably the ideal type for the beginner. As you progress, the projects you will want to undertake will obviously become larger in scale and a loom that will allow you to create larger items would be beneficial. However these larger looms are more expensive, so should only be purchased if you are truly dedicated and will gain full benefit from their use.

Shown here are a number of the looms that are available and on page 93 there is a list of suppliers that will be able to supply a loom suitable for the level of project you wish to undertake. All of the projects in this book can be completed using a simple wooden frame loom.

BEADS

Today, there is a huge choice of colourful beads and the choice is growing all the time. The main bead used in bead weaving is known as the seed bead, although in some beading catalogues they are described as glass Rocaille beads. They come in a variety of sizes and will be labelled with a size ranging from 22/0 to 1/0. This sizing is worked out by the number of beads there are to each inch (2.5cm) when they are laid out flat in a line. Therefore size 5/0 will be a bigger bead than say size 11/0, as size 5/0 you will only get 5 beads for every inch whilst for size 11/0 you will get 11 beads per inch.

The sizes frequently sold in shops and via catalogues tend to range from 5/0 to 11/0. The bead size used mostly for bead weaving is 11/0.

TIP

If you wish to make a larger piece yet do not have a large loom, you can weave several pieces and simply sew them together, edge-to-edge, to create a larger finished piece.

Seed beads in some of the colours available to the crafter today

As with many crafts, this is not a hard-and-fast rule so, if you find it difficult to weave using this size, perhaps you should use a 10/0 or 9/0. Obviously the size of bead you use will affect the finished size of your project. For the projects in this book I have used size 11/0 seed beads, unless otherwise stated in the Materials list for a specific project.

Using larger-sized beads opens up this craft to children, as they sometimes find it difficult to thread the smaller beads, and projects such as bracelets and necklaces can be fun for a child to undertake. Some craft suppliers prefer to sell just three sizes of beads, small, medium, or large and, in this case, the medium-size beads (size 11/0) would be the best for children.

The only problem with the seed beads is that they are slightly wider than they are long and, if you do not allow for this in the pattern you are using, your finished project will not be completely square. This can be overcome by using a type of bead called a Delicas, which has two advantages: firstly, they are as wide as they are long, allowing you to use alternate patterns (see Where to Obtain Further Inspiration, on page 91) and achieve a truer balance to your finished design; secondly, they have slightly larger holes, so beading is easier. The only drawback with them is that they are slightly more expensive than the regular seed beads, and with the larger projects you may need to take this into account.

A small selection of beads that may be mixed in when you are bead weaving

BEADING NEEDLE

The beading needle comes in a variety of lengths and eye types. Obviously the needle must be able to pass through the bead with ease and be long enough for the project being undertaken. If you have problems threading a particular needle, try using one with a larger eye than normal, and this should overcome the problem. As a simple rule of thumb, select a thin, straight needle which you are able to thread with ease and which will pass through your bead without any force.

THREAD

Thread is as important to the finished work as the beads you use. Try to ensure that you use a good beading thread for your weaving, i.e. one that is both thin and strong. A variety of threads with many different brand names are available on the market today, ranging from nylon to silk. However, the most important factor to take into consideration is that the thread is thin enough to pass through the bead twice. Also, try to ensure that the colour of thread you use blends with the colours in your design: if you are using dark colours, then try to avoid using a white thread; if your design consists of several colours, then pick the dominant colour and match your thread to that.

SCISSORS

Any pair of small, sharp scissors is fine for cutting the threads and I personally use a pair of good-quality nail scissors. I also colour-code all my craft scissors so that any member of the household using them for cutting something they should not knows that they are in trouble. Because of this, I do not find my fine thread-cutting scissors covered in glue, or other inappropriate things.

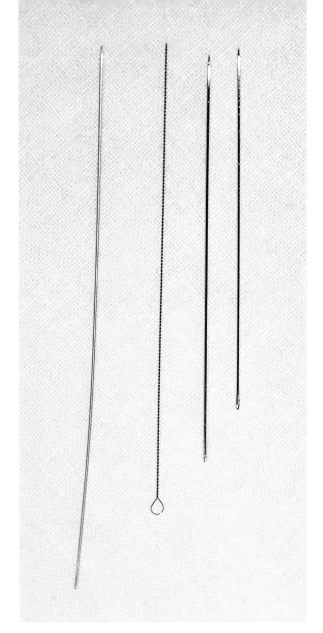

A selection of beading needles

Threads should be matched to the beads being used

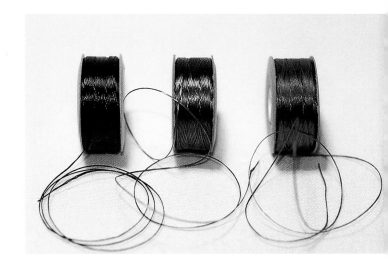

Ends of threads tied together and rolled around the holding spool

STICKY TAPE

One method for casting off your weaving requires the use of tape and the ideal type is a good-quality masking tape. Double-sided tape is also suitable, and this is used on the card projects later in this book.

SETTING UP YOUR LOOM

First decide upon the design or project you wish to create and count across the design to work out how many columns there are. If you find the design has 10 beads, then you will require 11 pieces of thread. As the beads sit between the threads that run the length of the loom, you will always require one extra thread to columns of beads.

The length of thread you will require is obviously determined by the item you are making, but always ensure that, in addition, you have plenty of thread over at each end of your project; this will make it easier to finish it off, especially if you are using Method Two (see page 16). As a guideline, I recommend a minimum of 15cm (6in) extra thread at each end of the project.

Once you have chosen the length of your threads, cut them and knot them together at one end. Place this onto one end of the loom by slipping it over the anchor – which is often simply a nail – on the holding spool. Roll the holding spool away from the loom, carefully wrapping the thread around the spool (see picture above).

Double threads on the outer edge for added strength

Fan the threads out so that each is within an adjacent notch, running down the centre section of your loom. Now tie the other end of your threads together and repeat the process at the opposite end of the loom, making sure that the threads are evenly spaced and that the tension is even across each one.

These threads are known as the warp threads (and will be described as such from now on). The warp threads should not sag in the middle of the loom, so make sure that they are sufficiently taut, yet not so tight that they break while you are weaving.

Once your warp threads are in position on your loom, you are ready to begin weaving.

NOTE

On projects which require a little more strength, I recommend using a double thread on the two outer warp threads, and I have specified this in the step-by-step sections of the relevant projects. For example, on a project that is five beads across, you would need the normal six warp threads plus the two extra threads, making a total of eight threads.

GETTING STARTED

ead weaving can be fiddly and setting yourself up in the following way prior to weaving should cut down on some of the more frustrating moments you may encounter.

⊙ Place your beads in easy-to-access containers, with a single colour in each one. Lids from old jars are ideal as they are deep enough to stop the beads from rolling away, yet large enough for the biggest of fingers. Also, with a low lip, they are less likely to get tipped over during use.

⊙ When first starting out you may find it easiest to work at a suitable table. However, I find it relaxing working on my lap, using a large flat tray, while watching one of the many easy-to-follow 'soaps' on television.

⊙ Ensure that you have good lighting, so that you do not strain your eyes while threading, weaving and reading the pattern.

⊙ Place any tools you will require, such as thread and a small pair of scissors, within easy reach of your loom.

⊙ If using Method One for casting off (see page 15), you will also need masking or double-sided tape, depending on which project you are working on.

BEGINNING TO WEAVE

Cut a piece of thread approximately 1m (around 1yd) in length and tie one end to the last thread on the loom, on the end nearest to you (see below). We will be working in such a way that the weaving grows away from you. However, if you find it easier to work the other way round, with the weaving growing towards you, then do so. I start with the furthest left-hand warp thread as

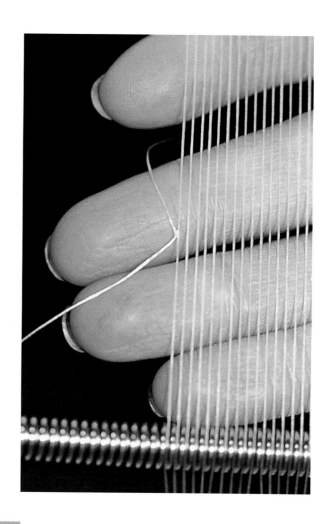

Weft thread tied onto outer warp thread

I am left-handed so, if you are right-handed, you may find it easier to work from right to left. There are no hard-and-fast rules and finding what suits you best will increase your enjoyment of this craft.

Once you have tied one end of the thread to the outside warp thread, pass the free end through your needle. You are now ready to begin weaving. The thread that is to be passed through the beads will travel from right to left, or left to right. It is known as the weft thread and will be called that from now on.

BASIC WEAVING INSTRUCTIONS

If you are working from the end of the loom nearest to you, then you will read the pattern from the bottom upwards. However if you prefer to work down towards you, then read the pattern from the top to the bottom. Placing the pattern in front of you and your beads within easy reach, consult the pattern and place the required beads on your needle.

Next, place the needle holding the beads under the warp threads. Using your other hand, push the beads up so that one bead sits between each warp thread (see top right). While still holding the beads in position, pull the needle through, followed by all the thread, then push the needle back through the holes of the beads. This time you must ensure that the weft thread runs over the warp threads, so that it holds the beads in place (see bottom right). Pull the thread tight, so that the beads are secured in position.

To secure the beads more firmly, prior to threading on your next row, wrap the weft thread around the outer warp thread just the once.

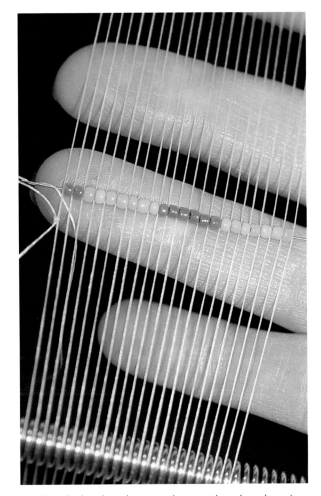

Pushing the beads up between the warp threads and passing the needle through for the first time

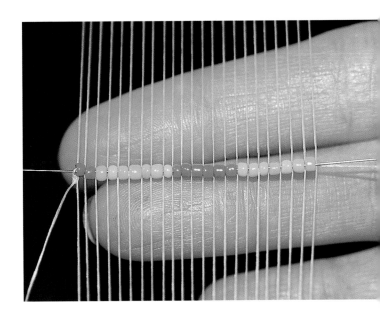

Passing the weft thread back through the beads over the top of the warp thread this time

Pull tightly on it and the weft thread will sit comfortably around the warp thread. Again, if you feel the item being made might need a little extra security against unravelling, as it is likely to take a lot of wear and tear, you could do this every other row.

JOINING A NEW THREAD

When the thread you are working with is near its end, simply tie it off and weave the end back through the last two rows of beads. Pull the thread tight and cut off the loose end. To attach a new thread, knot it to the outer thread, leaving a long loose end, and begin to weave as before. At some point this loose end must be woven into the beads and the end cut close to the weaving.

Knot off the weft thread around the warp thread

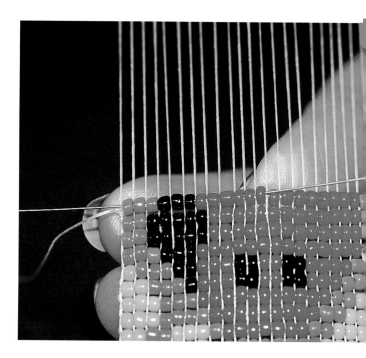

Pass the thread back through the beads and bring up in middle of row and cut off loose end

FINISHING/CASTING OFF

There are three methods of finishing off the weaving prior to removing it from the loom, and the method you use is governed by the type of project you are making. Method Two and Method Three are very similar (see instructions overleaf) and tend to be used for jewellery items, but the method you use depends upon the type of fixing you will be using.

METHOD ONE

For this you will need some good quality masking tape or double-sided sticky tape. It is quicker than Method Two and Three but is only suitable for projects where the reverse of the beading is not visible when complete.

Once your project is complete, take a piece of tape, place it under the threads and push it up so that it makes contact and sticks to the warp threads. Cut the tape flush with the threads. Leave approximately 1mm ($^1/_{32}$in) of the warp thread, to allow the tape to be pulled around to the back of your beaded project.

Now take a second piece of tape and repeat the process but on the top of the warp threads. Once all the warp threads are sandwiched between the tapes you can cut the threads to release your project from the loom.

If the design you have woven is to be placed on the front of a card or something similar, then double-sided sticky tape can be used instead. This will allow you to use the tape both for fastening off the threads and sticking the beaded project to your chosen surface.

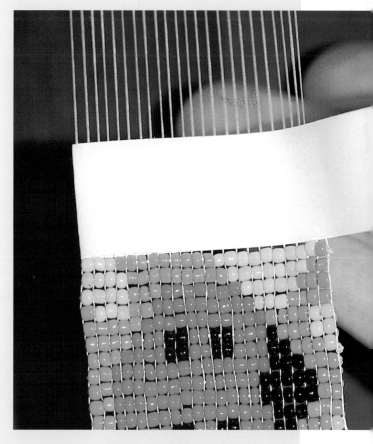

Tape wound around the warp threads prior to them being cut

METHOD TWO

This takes a little more time than Method One but is suitable for projects where both sides of the finished item are going to be on view, such as a necklace or similar piece of jewellery.

  Once the weaving is complete, release one end from the loom. Take two threads (the outermost thread and the one next to it) and knot them securely, then thread one of these strands onto your needle. Now begin to weave the thread through the centre of your beads until you have worked through several beads. Bring the thread out through the centre of a row and cut the thread close to the bead. Continue in this way until all the threads are knotted and then woven back through the beads and cut.

All ends knotted and joined together in the middle of the woven project (Method Three)

METHOD THREE

Knot off the two outer threads in the normal manner but, rather than weaving them back through the beads, simply pass them through the beads until they get to the centre of the weaving (see above). Continue in this fashion until all your threads are bunched together in the middle of the weaving, then knot all the threads together securely. This will allow you to use a necklet end, which is closed around the final knot (see left), which in turn will allow you to attach the correct jewellery finding to your finished woven project.

Necklet end placed around the knot, prior to being gently squeezed together with a pair of pliers (Method Three)

OTHER WEAVING TECHNIQUES

There are other weaving techniques that can be used on their own, or in conjunction with the basic weaving process. These are: open weaving; split weaving; adding texture by using different-sized beads; placing beads on the warp threads; increasing or decreasing the number of beads used per row, and fringing. These techniques may be fiddly, but can add an extra dimension to any finished item, so they are well worth learning and adding to your repertoire.

OPEN WEAVING

This type of weaving allows you to create holes within the weaving using large or long beads, such as the bugle bead. You use the same method as you would for the seed beads, but simply spread your warp threads further apart. This method can be used in conjunction with the basic bead weaving to create some really interesting effects.

SPLIT WEAVING

With this technique you don't weave a complete row from one end to the other, so you are able to create holes within the weaving which are only apparent when the weaving is pulled apart. It is a great method for creating holes suitable for slipping through a simple fastening, such as a bead or button. It can also be used to great effect if you wish to add interest to your project by overlapping some of the beading, as in the Glasses Cord project (see page 59).

Beginning to work split weaving

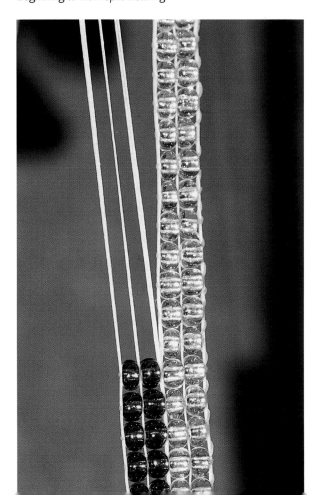

Continuing to work split weaving

DECREASING/INCREASING NUMBER OF BEADS PER ROW

Sometimes your project will require you to decrease or increase the number of beads you are weaving. As it is easier to decrease the number, it is advisable to work backwards when you want to increase. This may sound confusing, but I will explain.

If you have a length of weaving which requires you to work with nine beads per row and then taper down to one at either end, start with the full nine beads at one end. As you will be returning to this end later you must remember at this point to leave extra length on your thread. Work the required amount of rows and when you reach the other end, wrap your weft thread around the warp thread, then pass it back through the first bead. For the next row you must lose one bead at either end, so work just seven beads. Wrap your weft thread around the warp thread again and pass through the first bead as you did before. Now place five beads onto the needle and work in the normal manner. Continue in this way until you reach the last row, which has just the single bead. In this way you have decreased your beads. Now, to make it appear that you have increased your beads on the other end, roll back the loom so you return to your first row. Using the original thread you started to weave with, decrease the beads in the same manner. In this way it will appear that you have increased your beading when in fact you have decreased it.

USING DIFFERENT-SIZED OR SHAPED BEADS

Although in weaving it is nice to have a neat and even weave, you can add extra interest if you change the size of the bead you are weaving with between the rows. Although this method is not suitable if you are trying to create an image within your weaving, mixed beads can be used to great effect with designs that rely on texture

Beads placed on the warp thread prior to weaving

and colour rather than image. It is also a great way to use up odd beads left over from a previous project that are not enough to use for an image project.

PLACING BEADS ON THE WARP THREADS

Beads do not have to follow the direction of the weft thread – they can also be integrated into the project design and follow the warp thread. This is done during the setting up of the loom. Cut your required threads in the normal manner and knot one end. Now take one of the threads and thread through your beading needle. Place the required number of your chosen beads onto the thread. Work through all of the warp threads in this way until each has the number of beads required for your design (see picture above). Now knot the loose ends together. Put the warp thread onto the loom as you would for any other weaving project, placing the beads between the spacer bar and the roller until they are required by your design. When you need to use them within the project, simply loosen the tension slightly on your warp thread, then slide them over the spacer bar and weave into your design.

FRINGING

There are two types of fringing that can be added to the edge of your weaving: the hanging fringe creates long strands of beads which look wonderful when allowed to hang down and sway, while the looped fringe creates small loops of beads along the outer edges.

HANGING FRINGE

A hanging fringe can be added during the weaving process and become an integral part of it. You work a row in the normal manner but, prior to working the next row, you create your fringing. To do this, thread on the required number of beads, then thread the needle through the beads from the second bead upwards. In this way the first, or end, bead will ensure that the other beads are anchored in place. Take the needle through all the beads and pull your thread tight. To ensure the thread is then secured, wrap it once around the outer warp thread and pull tightly again. You can then work on your next row of beading. Continue in this fashion until you have created a fringe that will move during wear, which looks great on all manner of items from bags to necklaces (see top right).

LOOPED FRINGE

This is a simple method of adding a little interest and texture but, unlike the hanging fringe, it is worked after the weaving is finished. You can either add a looped fringe while the weaving is still on the loom, or you can cast off your piece, then work on it without the constraints of the loom. I prefer the latter method, as it enables me to move the woven piece around with ease.

A hanging fringe adds interest and movement

Small loop fringing adds fine detail and texture

To create the looped fringe, cut a piece of thread and tie it to the outermost warp thread. Place four beads on your needle and then pass the needle through the warp thread on the third row. Pull it tight, so the beads create a small loop along the outer edge. Place another four beads on the thread and again, miss one line and pass the thread through the next row. Continue in this fashion, working alternate rows each time.

NOTE

When creating a looped fringe, it's advisable to work from one end to the other, then work the other side in the same direction. In this way the fringing will lay in the same direction on the two sides, creating a more even appearance to your finished piece.

HINTS AND TIPS FOR BETTER WEAVING

• Try to ensure that the tension on the weft threads is even. This will come with practice: too tight and your piece will be very stiff; too loose and the beads will not sit comfortably together.

• Also try to ensure that all your beads are the same size – even with today's manufacturing techniques some beads, which are not quite as wide or as long as the other beads, slip through the net. If you use a bead which is not a uniform size, then it will make your finished piece of work look uneven. However do not throw these beads away as they can be used in experimental pieces, for example where you want to create interest with texture, or different-shaped or sized beads. However, if you come across a bead which has a hole that is small and/or uneven, it is best to throw it away.

• As you will be passing the thread through the holes of the beads a minimum of two times, always try to use the thinnest, strongest thread you can for your project.

• If you find it difficult to pass the thread through the bead, try waxing the thread. Waxing blocks are available from many goods suppliers of beading equipment but, if you do not have a waxing block, then a candle will do the job just as well. When I was weaving items for this book, I ensured that I was using good quality thread, which passed through the beads without fraying or breaking, so I had no need of wax.

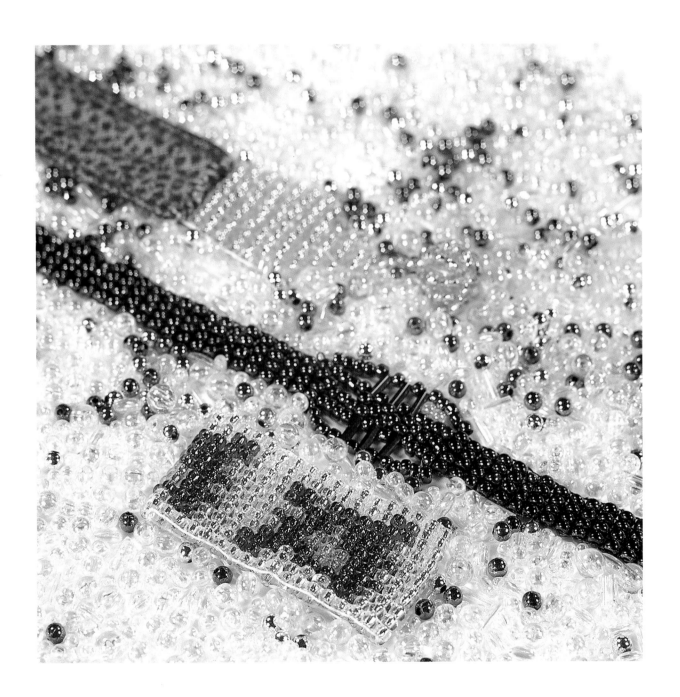

Happy
Christmas

THE PROJECTS

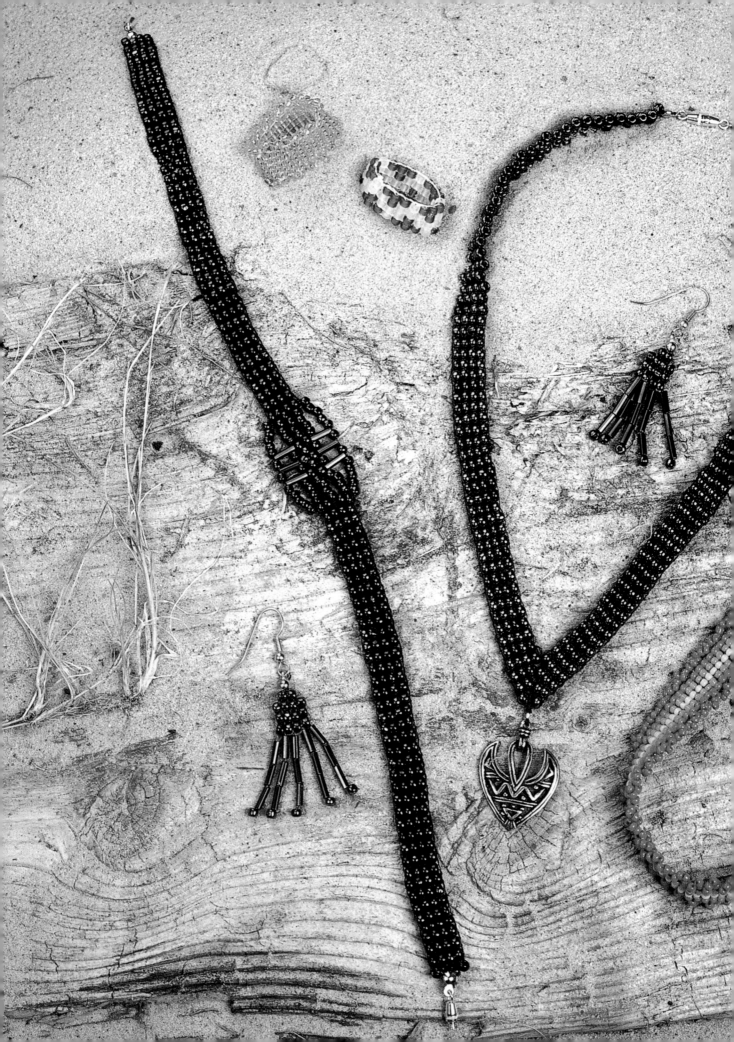

JEWELLERY

Jewellery can be used to dress up
an outfit or simply to add a little fun.
Whichever way you choose to use
jewellery, it is an important part of any
wardrobe and can be used to say
a lot about you. With a simple
change of colour any of the following
designs will fit in with your wardrobe
and allow you to make that
'personal' statement.

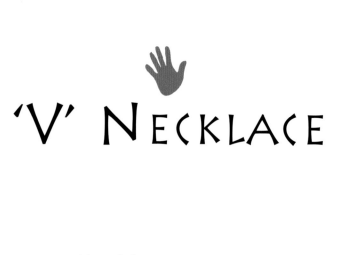

'V' Necklace

We all love to wear something a little different from the crowd when we dress up and this necklace is sure to get you noticed. It uses the basic bead-weaving technique with a little decreasing, so is an ideal project for the beginner.

METHOD

1 Set up your loom with five warp threads each 55cm (22in) long.

2 Cast on your weft thread leaving a free strand, approximately 15cm (6in) long, and thread through the needle.

3 Weave 60 rows of four beads following the basic weave section.

MATERIALS

You will need basic materials (see page 6) plus

Seed beads (size 11/0) x 496
Large accent bead/pendant (see photograph for idea of size and type)
Crimp ring x 1
Necklet ends x 2
Clasp (bullet type used in sample shown)
Pliers

---

4 On row 61 weave just three beads. Decrease this to two beads on the next row and one on the last.

5 Leave the loose threads on this end of your weaving for now.

6 Return to the first row and weave just two beads in front of your first row.

7 Cast off your warp threads using Method Three (see page 16) and end with a large knot in the centre of the last two beads.

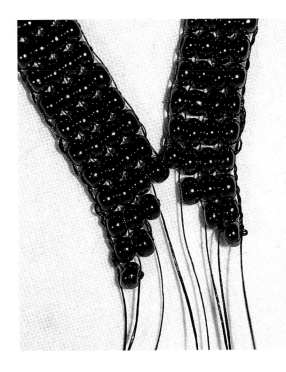

Tying the warp threads of the tapered end of the necklace (step 10)

All ends tied off and knotted together (step 10)

8 Remove your weaving from the loom.

9 To weave the other side of your necklace, repeat this process, following steps 1 to 7.

10 Once you have woven both halves of the necklace, join the tapered ends together by knotting the threads (see photographs above). Weave back through the beads and cut all the threads apart from the middle four, which come from the point of the necklace.

11 Thread these last four threads through a crimp ring, as shown on the right.

12 Thread your accent bead/pendant onto these four threads and pass back up through the crimp ring.

Warp threads threaded through crimp ring and pendant (step 11)

Squeezing the crimp ring to close with pliers (step 13)

13 Use the pliers to squeeze the crimp ring as shown on the right, then thread the loose ends through the beads, then cut the loose ends.

14 To complete the necklace, close a necklet end around the large knot and attach the bullet clasp.

NOTE

To make your necklace a little stronger, add an extra warp thread on each side, so that you have two warp threads on each outer edge.

BRACELET

B racelets are a great
fashion accessory and can be
worn alone, or as part of a grouping of
three or four. So why not be a little different and
wear a bracelet no-one else will have. Even if you
follow this pattern to the letter, no two bracelets will
ever be the same, as we all have our idiosyncracies.

METHOD

1 Cut eight warp threads 50cm (20in) long and
set up your loom in the normal manner, using
two threads on the outer edges of the
weaving for strength.

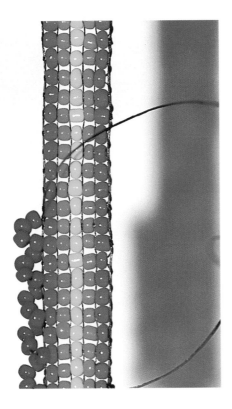

MATERIALS

You will need basic materials (see page 6) plus

Necklet ends x 2
Clasp
Pliers
Seed beads (size 11/0) in following colours:
Colour A (yellow) x 70
Colour B (orange) x 140
Colour C (light red) x 140
Colour D (dark red) x 290

2 Weave 70 rows, placing the beads on your
needle in the following order: Colour C – B
– A – B – C.

3 Once you have woven the required number
of rows, knot off your weft thread and weave
it back into the beads.

Beginning to create the fringed edging (step 4, overleaf)

4 To create the looped fringe, cut a new piece of thread approximately 60cm (24in) long and attach it to the two outer threads. Place four colour 'D' beads onto this thread, then go along two rows and catch into the weaving by wrapping around the outer warp thread. Continue in this fashion until you have created a looped fringe down the side of the weaving (see the lower picture on the previous page). For further instructions on looped fringes, see page 19.

5 Repeat this process along the second edge, working in the same direction as the first side, to ensure an even appearance.

6 Once your weaving is complete, cast off your threads using Method Three (see page 16).

7 Attach the necklet ends and the clasp to complete (see picture on the facing page).

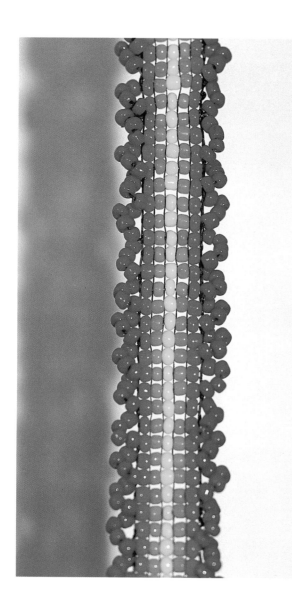

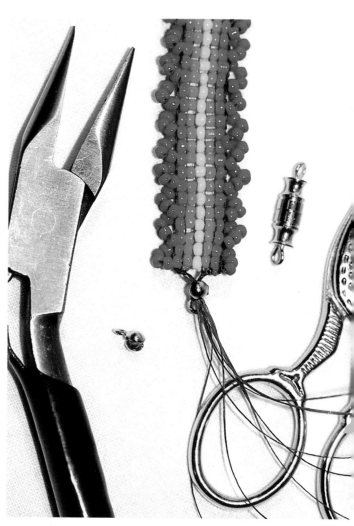

The warp threads tied and knotted, and the necklet end placed around knot (step 7)

The completed fringe (step 5)

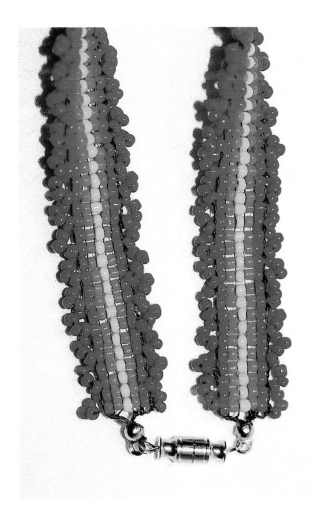

The bullet clasp fitted and the bracelet complete

METHOD FOR BRACELET WITHOUT A CLASP

To create a bracelet without a clasp, which simply pushes over the hand, add the following number of seed beads (size 11/0) to the number detailed above:

Colour A (yellow) x 10
Colour B (orange) x 20
Colour C (light red) x 20
Colour D (dark red) x 80

When complete, remove from the loom, wrap it back around upon itself and securely knot each corresponding thread. Once the threads are knotted, weave any loose ends back through the beads and cut the threads close to the beads.

NOTE

If the bracelet is for someone with a small wrist, weave fewer rows. It is always best to measure the required length and work to that, rather than find the finished item is too big and keeps slipping off.

RINGS

I f, like me, you tend to talk with your hands, there can be no jewellery more visible than the ring. The type of ring you wear can be as individual as you are, and the great thing about these fun rings is that they take very few beads. They are also really quick to make, allowing you to create a range that will surely fit with any outfit you have hanging in your wardrobe.

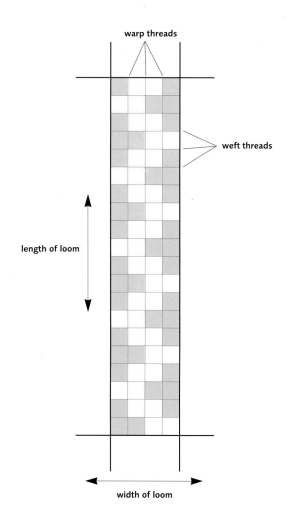

warp threads

weft threads

length of loom

width of loom

Bead-weaving pattern for Version One

VERSION ONE: FROSTED RING

METHOD

1 Set up your loom with five threads in the normal manner, each thread 35cm (14in) in length, or at least as long as the loom.

2 Weave the ring, following the pattern shown.

3 Remember that the ring must be able to slide over the knuckle so, once complete, check that it will fit the finger it is to be worn on.

4 Once you are happy that the ring will fit, remove the ring from the loom, bring the piece of weaving around on itself so that it creates a tube, then tie off the threads (see picture on right). Once tied off, weave the loose ends back through the beads and cut off any unwanted ends.

If you wish to add a fringe to the Version One ring this can easily be done by following the method used for Version Two, steps 4 and 5, but alternating the two bead colours on the thread creating the looped fringe.

Casting off the ends by tying off corresponding threads (step 4)

VERSION TWO: SINGLE-COLOUR RING WITH LOOPED FRINGE

METHOD

1 Set up your loom with six threads in the normal manner. The threads should be 35cm (14in) in length, or at least as long as the loom.

2 Weave the required number of rows to create a ring long enough to fit around the finger it is to be worn on.

MATERIALS

You will need

Seed beads (size 11/0) in your chosen colour, approximately 200

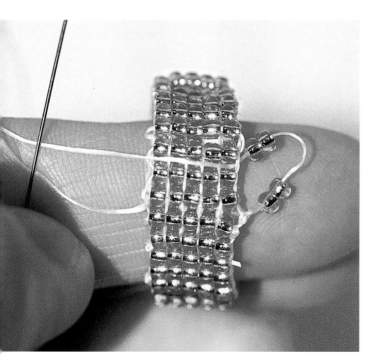

Creating the small loop fringe along the outer edge (step 4)

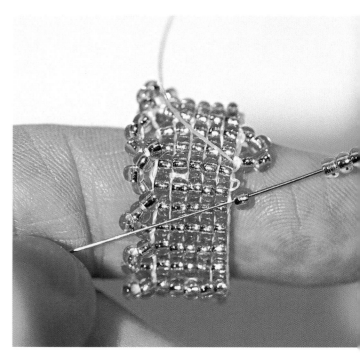

Working the looped fringe along the opposite side in the same manner (step 5)

3 Cast off using Method Two (see page 16) but do not cut the two outer threads yet.

4 Using one of the outer threads, create a looped fringe around the chosen edge of your ring. To do this, place four beads on the thread, then catch in every other row (see pictures above).

5 Fasten off the thread, then repeat the process on the other edge.

NOTE

This simple design can be scaled up to create a lovely napkin ring, or scaled up even further to create a bracelet.

CHOKER

This choker uses a variety of techniques and is great for either funky day wear or classy evening wear, depending upon the type of beads you choose to use.

METHOD

1 Cut five 60cm (24in) warp threads and knot together just the one end.

2 Thread the warp threads with seed beads before placing them on the loom. The two warp threads on the outer edge will require 12 beads each, while the middle warp threads will require 10 beads each.

3 Once the seed beads are threaded onto the warp threads, knot the ends and set up your loom, ensuring that the two threads with 12 beads are on the two outside edges.

4 Cast on your weft thread and weave 41 rows.

5 Now bring down along your warp thread five seed beads on the two outer edge threads and four seed beads on the middle three threads.

6 Run your weft thread along the inside of the five seed beads on the outer warp thread.

MATERIALS

You will need basic materials (see page 6) plus

Bugle beads, 6mm (¹/₄in) x 6
Seed beads (size 11/0) x 392
Necklet ends x 2
Clasp
Pliers

TIP

Before starting to weave, check that you have placed the seed beads threaded on the warp threads at the end you are working towards. There is nothing more frustrating than finding that you have placed the beads at the wrong end of the loom, so that you are unable to bring them down into place.

First row of open weaving using bugle beads (step 7)

Continuing with the open weaving (above step 9, below step13)

7 Now open weave into your design your next row, which comprises one bugle bead, two seed beads and one bugle bead.

8 Bring down one seed bead on each of the warp threads.

9 Weave your next row, repeating step 7.

10 Pull down another one seed bead along each warp thread.

11 Repeat step 7.

12 Bring down the last of the seed beads on your warp threads. There should be five on the outer threads and four on the inner threads.

13 Now weave 41 rows of basic weaving.

14 Cast off using Method Three (see page 16).

15 To complete the choker, attach the findings.

Ends of necklace finished with clasp (step 15)

EARRINGS

Earrings can make or break any look you are trying to create – they can add a little sophistication, or they can be more frivolous. Whichever you prefer, these earrings are sure to fit the bill and, with a little alteration to the colour of beads used, they will work well as either day or evening wear. The added bonus is that they are very quick to make, so make an ideal gift for family and friends.

METHOD

1 Cut five threads 35cm (14in) long and knot the one end.

2 Place three bugle beads, then one seed bead on each of the five threads (shown right).

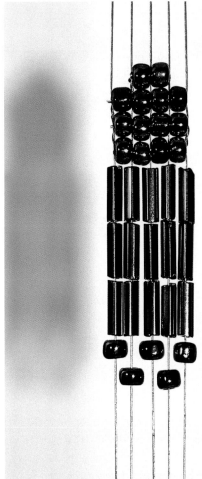

Basic weaving complete, and beads on the warp threads brought up ready to work (step 2)

3 Knot the second end and place on the loom.

4 Weave three rows of four beads, then position a fourth row of just two beads centrally.

5 Fasten off your weft thread.

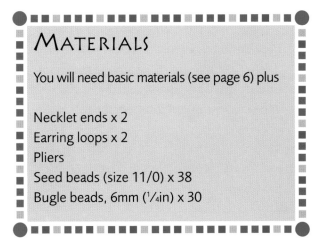

MATERIALS

You will need basic materials (see page 6) plus

Necklet ends x 2
Earring loops x 2
Pliers
Seed beads (size 11/0) x 38
Bugle beads, 6mm (¼in) x 30

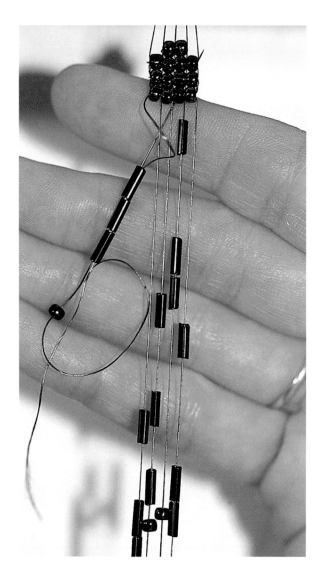

The first tassel being worked (step 6)

Three of the tassels completed (step 9)

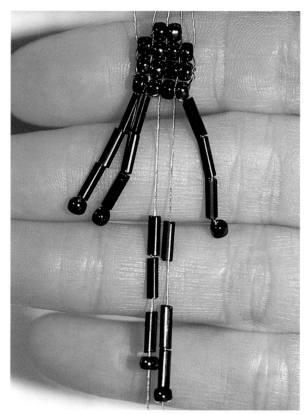

6 Take one of the warp strands which you threaded with three bugle beads and a seed bead in step 2, and push the beads up, so that a bugle bead is next to the piece you have just woven. Release just the one warp thread from the loom.

7 Thread this through a needle, then pass it through the bugle beads. In this fashion the seed bead is used to stop the bugle beads coming off the end of the thread.

8 Pass the thread through the outer seed bead on the first row of weaving. Knot around the top of the warp thread, then pass the thread back down the middle of the bugle beads once again. Knot a second time around the warp thread. Pass back up through the bugle beads and come out after the second bead. Cut the end of the loose thread close to the bead.

9 Repeat this process for the other four warp threads.

Weaving complete, apart from adding the findings (step 10)

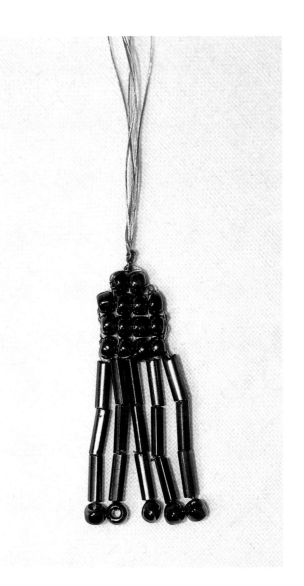

10 Cast off the other end of the weaving using Method Three (see page 16).

11 To complete the earring, crimp the necklet end around the knot, cut loose ends and attach the ear wire.

12 Repeat the process to make the second earring.

NOTE

When working these earrings, remember that the first row must be at the end of the loom where you have placed the beads on the warp threads, otherwise these beads will end up at the wrong end of the weaving. Also remember that the seed bead must be the one furthest away from the weaving.

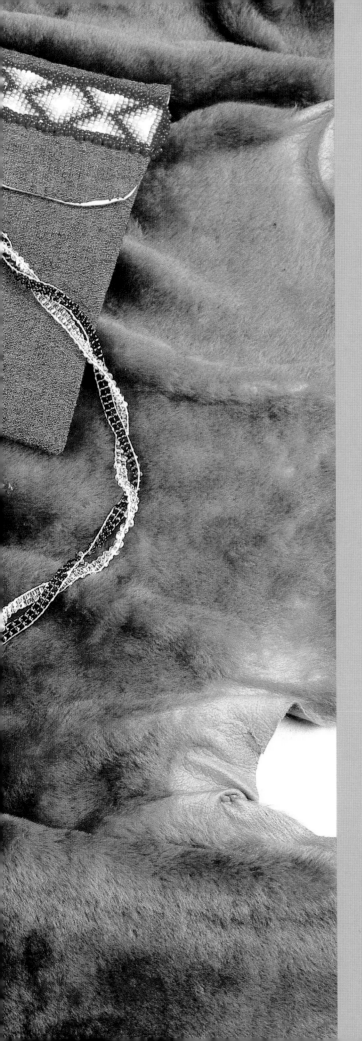

ACCESSORIES

Whatever your age, the right
accessories are as important as the
clothes you wear, and the great thing
about them is that they reflect your
style, and show the world exactly who
you are. So make a statement and be
seen with the following projects – all
can be adapted to suit your individual
taste and colour preferences.

PURSE

The purse is a very individual item and one that is carried with you everywhere. It can say a lot about you, so show just how creative you can be with and this delightful beaded fish motif.

METHOD FOR SEWING PURSE

1 Cut out the following pieces of fabric (see 'Note' about selvage on page 45):
(**A**) 15 x 31cm (6 x 12½in) x 2
(**B**) 15 x 13cm (6 x 5in) x 2
(**C**) 13 x 8cm (5 x 3in) x 1
(**D**) 15 x 14cm (6 x 5½in) x 1

2 Place one piece of '**A**' fabric to one side – this will become piece '**A1**'.

3 Take both pieces of '**B**' fabric, double-turn just one of the longer edges of each one, turning in 6mm (¼in) twice, and sew the seam into place. One piece will now become '**B1**' and the other '**B2**'.

4 Pin the un-sewn long edge of piece '**B1**' along one of the shorter edges of piece '**A2**'.

5 Take piece '**C**' and create a seam by turning in 6mm (¼in) twice along one of the longer edges, then sew the seam into place.

6 Make one 6mm (¼in) fold along each of the two shorter edges of piece '**C**' and pin the folds in place. Place the longer, unturned

MATERIALS

You will need basic materials (see page 6) plus

Seed beads (size 11/0) in the following colours:

Blue x 23
Red x 144
Black x 176
Light green x 142
Dark green x 154
Denim fabric or heavyweight cotton fabric: 0.25m (10in)
Bias binding in matching colour: 12mm (½in) wide x 65cm (26in)
Basic sewing equipment plus:
Fabric scissors
Tailor's chalk
Buttons x 2
Sewing machine

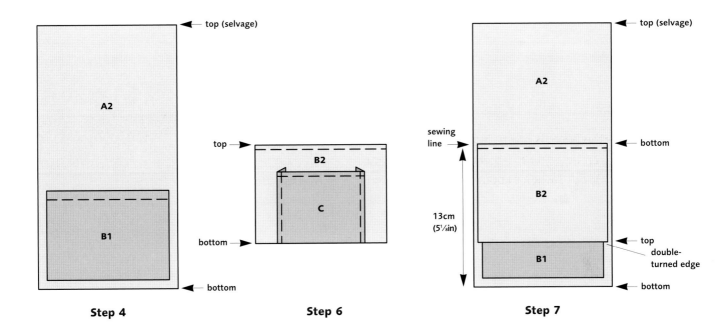

top (selvage)

A2

B1

bottom

Step 4

top →

B2

C

bottom →

bottom

Step 6

top (selvage)

A2

sewing line

bottom

B2

13cm (5¼in)

B1

top
double-turned edge

bottom

Step 7

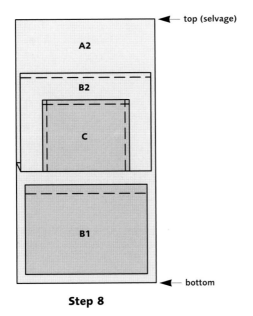

top (selvage)

A2

B2

C

B1

bottom

Step 8

edge of piece '**C**' centrally on the un-sewn edge of piece '**B2**', then sew down the two short pinned sides of piece '**C**', to create a small, open-ended pocket.

7 Following the diagram, turn piece '**B2**' face down and upside down (so that piece '**C**' is underneath) and align what is now the raw bottom edge of '**B2**' with the line marked 'sewing line 1', which is 13cm (5in) up from the bottom, shorter edge of '**A2**'. Sew along this line.

8 Fold piece '**B2**' back up, so the raw edge you have just sewn is hidden under the piece itself, and pockets '**C**' and '**B1**' are revealed again.

9 Pin the side edges of piece '**B2**' in place, to form a pocket.

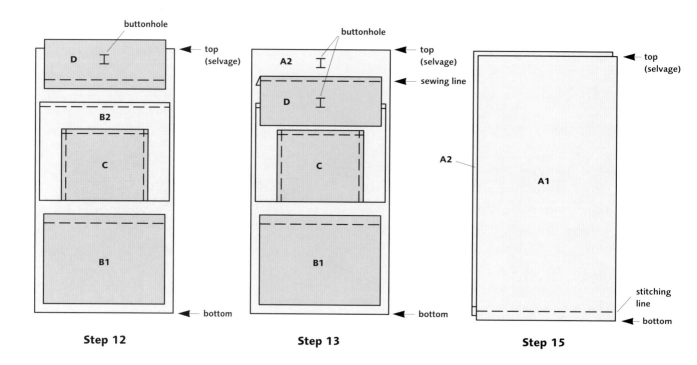

buttonhole

top
(selvage)

D

B2

C

B1

bottom

Step 12

buttonhole

top
(selvage)

sewing line

A2

D

C

B1

bottom

Step 13

top
(selvage)

A2

A1

stitching
line

bottom

Step 15

10 Take piece '**D**', and fold it in half lengthways, right sides together, so that it now measures 15 x 7cm (6 x 2³⁄₄in). Sew down the two shorter side edges. Snip the corners then turn inside out, so that the right side of the fabric is now on the outside.

11 To fasten the purse, either create a central buttonhole along the folded edge of piece '**D**', or fit a decorative press stud.

12 Place piece '**D**' as shown on the diagram and sew along 'sewing line 2', which is 4cm (1¹⁄₂in) from the raw edge of piece '**A2**'.

13 Fold piece '**D**' back on itself, so the raw edge is hidden, and sew a second line of straight stitches to hold this flap in place. If using a button fastening (see step 11) sew a button onto piece '**B2**' to align with the buttonhole on piece '**D**', and form a closed pocket. Alternatively, attach a press stud, or secure with a zip or piece of Velcro, for added security.

14 Place piece '**A2**' on top of piece '**A1**', right sides together, so the pockets are sandwiched in between.

15 Join '**A1**' and '**A2**' together with a straight line of sewing, 1cm (³⁄₈in) in from the lower shorter edge where piece '**B**' is attached.

16 Fold piece '**A2**' back, so the wrong sides of '**A1**' and '**A2**' are now together and the pockets revealed, then sew a line of straight stitching 6mm (¹⁄₄in) in from the edge, to hold it in place, as shown.

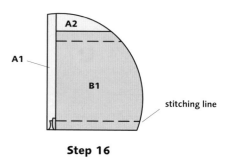

A2

A1

B1

stitching line

Step 16

17 Pin the long sides of pieces '**A1**' and '**A2**', so that they are level with each other.

18 Cut the bias binding in half, so you have two equal lengths of 32.5cm (13in). Open one folded edge of bias binding and pin it into position down one of the longer edges of the purse. Using the fold line as a guide, sew down the entire length of the purse side, to secure the bias binding in place. Fold the bias binding over the raw edge of the purse. Using the machine stitching as a guide, hand stitch the bias binding in place. In this way the raw edges of the purse are hidden and protected under the bias binding. Repeat this process for the other side.

19 Sew a second buttonhole centrally in the edge that will act as a flap when the purse is closed. (See step 11 for an alternative method of fastening.)

Bias binding trim along the side edges of the purse (step 18)

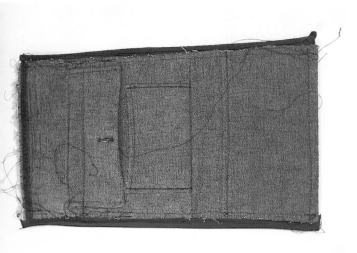

20 Fold the purse up, pocket-side inwards, using the tops of pieces '**B1**' and '**D**' as your guide for the folds. The top flap with the buttonhole should now overlap the bottom section. Attach a button or stud in line with your buttonhole (or press stud) to secure the purse.

NOTE

In the sample shown both '**A**' pieces were cut so the selvage (the non-fraying edge of the fabric) was part of one of the shorter ends, thus creating an interesting edge.

Optional bead fringing around the motif (step 5)

THE BEAD WEAVING

1 Cut 26 pieces of thread to a minimum length of 40cm (16in) and place on the loom in the normal manner.

2 Weave the design, following the chart below.

3 When the beaded motif is complete, cast off using Method Two (see page 16).

4 Once it is removed from the loom, position the motif beneath the flap on the front of the purse, and hand-stitch all the way around the outer edge of the motif, to secure it in place.

5 If you wish, you can add some looped fringing around the outer edge of the motif, to hide any untidy stitching (for instructions, see page 19).

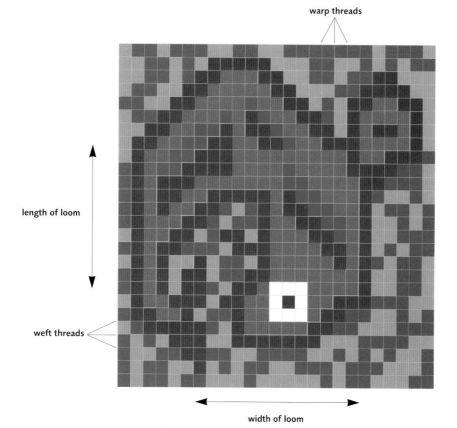

warp threads

Bead-weaving pattern

length of loom

weft threads

width of loom

GLASSES CASE

METHOD FOR SEWING THE CASE

1 Cut your outer and lining fabrics to the sizes given below right.

2 Take the piece of fabric for the outside of your case, and measure 15cm (6in) up from one of the shorter ends. Fold the fabric at this point, with right sides together, and align the edges. Sew the sides down, with a seam allowance of 1.5cm (⅝in) from the edge of the fabric, to form a pocket (see picture overleaf). Repeat this process with the lining fabric.

MATERIALS

You will need basic materials (see page 6) plus

Seed beads (size 11/0) in the following colours:
White x 57
Yellow x 108
Light blue x 183
Dark blue x 398
Outer fabric 12 x 46cm (4½ x 18in)
Lining fabric 12 x 46cm (4½ x 18in)
Basic sewing equipment plus:
Tailor's chalk
Sewing machine
Press stud

3 If the seam edges are rough, neaten them with a zigzag stitch.

4 Turn both pieces of fabric round the right way, to reveal two pockets with flaps.

5 Place the lining and the outer fabric together and align the longer sides.

Turning the unfinished edge, ready for sewing by hand (step 9)

6 Sew around the top tab, between the two seam lines, in a curved line.

7 Trim off the extra fabric.

8 Turn the top around to the right side and tuck the lining into the outer fabric, then iron along the sewing line.

9 Turn the unfinished top edge of the case in slightly and hand stitch into place.

10 Work out where you wish to position the press stud under the flap and sew into place.

Sewing down both sides of the outer layer and lining (step 2)

Sewing a curved line around the tab between the two seam lines (step 6)

The press stud sewn in place (step 10)

Bead-weaving pattern

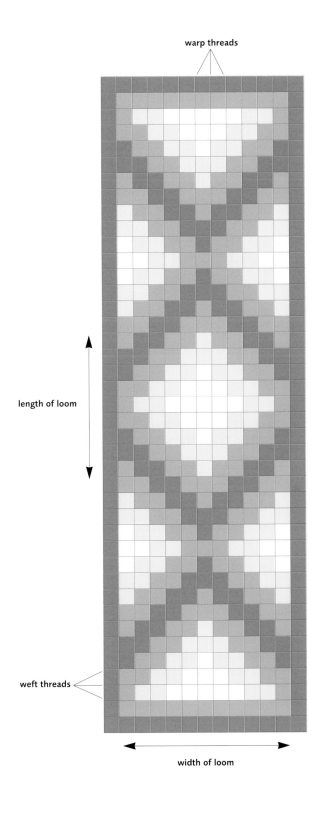

warp threads

length of loom

weft threads

width of loom

METHOD FOR WEAVING THE BEAD MOTIF

1 Cut 14 pieces of thread 40cm (16in) and set up loom in normal manner.

2 Weave the motif, following the pattern shown on the left.

3 Create a looped fringe down both long sides of the weaving (see instructions on page 19).

4 Cast off using Method Two (see page 16).

TO COMPLETE THE CASE

1 Place woven piece onto the flap of your glasses case and, using matching cotton, sew all the way around the outer edge.

2 When the woven motif is sewn in place, create a looped fringe along both shorter sides to create a more pleasing finish.

Beginning to create small loop fringing along the edge (step 3)

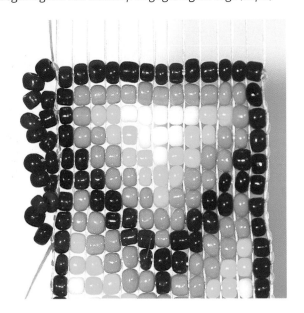

Woven section in place and completing the looped fringe (step 2)

Back of the completed project, with flap up

The completed project, with flap in closed position

HAIR CLIPS

If you have taken the trouble to put your hair up and need something to add a finishing touch, these two hair clips are sure to solve the problem. Version One is suitable for a more formal occasion, while Version Two is ideal for wearing out in the summer sun.

VERSION ONE

METHOD

1 Cut 13 threads at least 40cm (16in) long.

2 Knot one end and thread three bugle beads onto each thread.

3 Knot the other end and place on the loom in the normal manner.

MATERIALS

Version One
You will need basic materials (see page 6) plus

Bugle beads, 6mm ($1/4$in) x 39
Large seed beads (size 11/0) x 120
Small seed beads (size 14/0) x 112
Hair clasp backing
Small piece of white cotton fabric
Heavyweight interfacing
Fabric scissors
HB pencil

4 Then begin to bead as follows:
1st Row: 12 large beads
2nd Row: 12 small beads
3rd to 5th Row: 12 large beads
6th Row: 12 small beads
7th Row: Bring one bugle bead down into position on each thread
8th Row: 12 small beads
9th Row: Bring down a further bugle bead on each thread
10th Row: 12 small beads
11th Row: Bring down the last of the bugle beads
12th Row: 12 small beads
13th to 15th Row: 12 large beads
16th Row: 12 small beads
17th Row: 12 large beads
18th Row: Begin to decrease using just ten small beads centrally
19th Row: Continue to decrease with eight large beads
20th Row: Four small beads
21st Row: Four large beads
22nd Row: Four small beads and knot off your weft thread.

5 Return to the first row and decrease as you did for row 18 to row 22, then cast off the finished weaving using Method Two (see instructions on page 16).

COMPLETING THE HAIR CLIP:

1 Place the finished weaving on the heavyweight interfacing and draw around it.

2 Carefully cut out the interfacing, just inside the pencil mark.

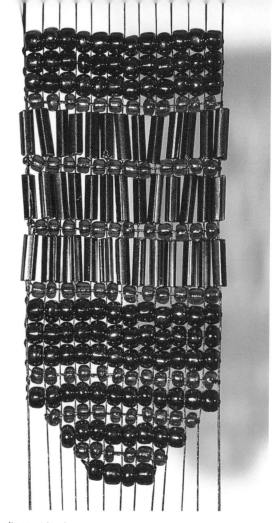

Hair-clip weaving in progress

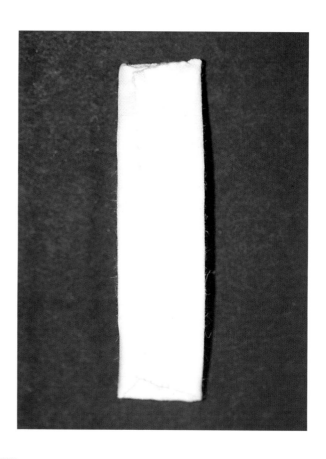

Cotton sewn around the stiff interfacing (step 4, facing page)

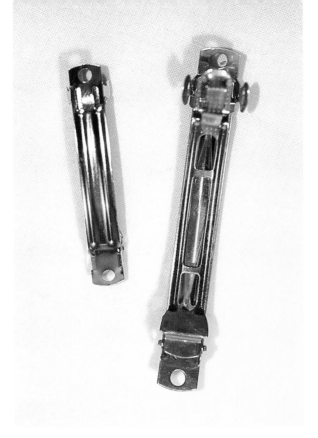

Hair-clasp backings

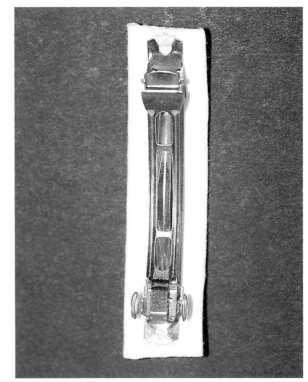

Hair-clasp backing sewn onto cotton backing (step 5)

3 Place the interfacing on the fabric and cut around it leaving approximately 1cm (^{3}/$_4$ in) around the edge.

4 Thread up a needle and fold the fabric around the interfacing, sewing in place as you go.

5 Once the interfacing is covered, turn over and sew the hair-clasp backing into position. Place centrally, along the middle of the fabric.

6 Now carefully position the beading and sew all the way around the outer edge to fix it in place. Use a thread that matches the beading, rather than the backing, as only the beading side of the clip will be seen during wear.

Hair-clasp backing sewn onto cotton backing

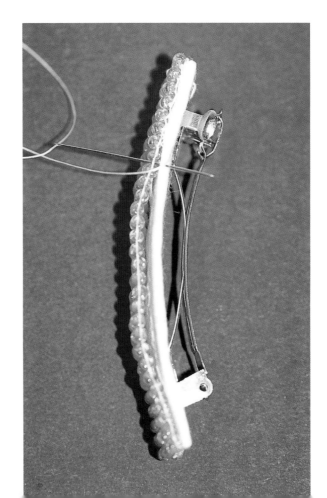

VERSION TWO

METHOD

1 To create this design, thread your loom up with ten threads each 40cm (16in) long.

2 Then, using the basic beading method and the pattern provided, weave your design.

3 To complete the backing and sew the beading onto the hair clasp, follow the 'Completing the hair clip' instructions given for Version One.

MATERIALS

Version Two
You will need the following beads

Colour A x 172 (yellow in sample shown)
Colour B x 83 (red in sample shown)

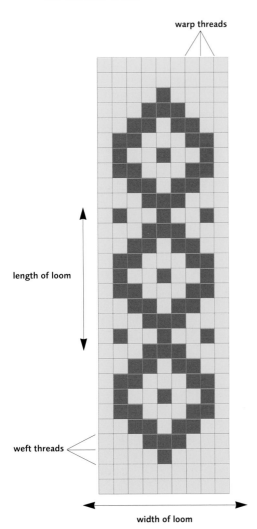

Bead-weaving pattern for Version Two

EVENING CLUTCH BAG

METHOD FOR SEWING THE BAG:

1 Neaten the raw edges of the fabric, if required, with a zigzag stitch.

2 Take the outer fabric and measure 16cm (6½in) up from the 43cm (16½in) edge. Fold the fabric along this line, right sides together. Align the edges and sew seams 1cm (⅜in) in from the edge of both sides, to create a pocket with a flap. Repeat the process with the lining.

Fabric folded and sewn down both sides (step 2)

MATERIALS

You will need basic materials (see page 6) plus

Outer fabric 21 x 43cm (8 x 16½in)
(I used black velvet)
Lightweight lining fabric (e.g. silk) 21 x 43cm (8 x 16½in)
Seed beads (size 11/0) x 700
Basic sewing equipment plus:
Fabric scissors
Tailor's chalk
Sewing machine
Large press stud
1m (1yd) of thick matching cord (if desired)

Flap sewn from seam to seam (step 4)

3 Turn both pieces around the right way.

4 Place the lining and outer fabric together, with the longest sides aligned, and sew from one seam to the other, around what will become the flap of the bag (see picture top right).

5 Turn the two fabrics right side out, tuck the lining 'pocket' into the outer fabric 'pocket', and iron the flap flat along the sewing line.

6 Turn the unfinished top edge of the bag slightly and hand stitch into place.

7 Work out the position of your press stud and hand stitch in place under the flap.

Top unfinished seam folded and pinned ready for hand stitching (step 6)

Weaving the fringe

CREATING BEADED FRINGING

1 Cast on five 46cm (18½in) threads and weave just three lines of basic weave.

2 On row four, begin to weave the long fringing, following the instructions for a hanging fringe on page 19. Increase the number of beads per row by one until you have worked 26 rows.

3 Now decrease the number of beads in the fringing per row by one until you have worked another 26 rows.

4 To complete, work three rows of basic weaving, then cast off using Method Two (see page 16).

Passing the needle back through the fringing

Knotting the thread to ensure it stays in position

TO COMPLETE THE BAG

1 Sew the beaded section into place with a neat hand stitch.

2 Finish by adding a small number of beads randomly on the main body of the bag.

3 The sample shown does not have a handle or strap but, if you would like to add one, sew a thick matching cord into position on either side, once the bag is complete.

Fringing in place with a scattering of beads

Glasses Cord

How many times have you put your glasses down, then spent the next half-hour looking for them? This easily made cord can be created in a range of colours that will tone or blend with your wardrobe, and will solve that problem.

Method:

1 Cut ten warp threads, each measuring 90cm (36in), and set up your loom placing two threads on the outer edges and four in the middle so that, running from one side to the other, you will have 2 – 1 – 4 – 1 – 2 threads. (Although this may look a little strange, all will become clear as you weave).

2 Cast on your weft threads and weave in four beads, two in colour '**A**' and two in colour '**B**'.

3 Continue in this way until you have ten rows, forming the solid piece of cord at each end.

4 Now split the warp threads into two equal sections, each with 2 – 1 – 2 warp threads.

5 Using the first five threads which have two columns of beads, weave just two of colour '**A**' beads until you have 180 rows.

6 Repeat this process with colour **B**.

Materials

You will need basic materials (see page 6) plus

Necklet ends x 2
Glasses holders x 2
Seed beads (size 11/0):
Colour A x 400
Colour B x 400
Pliers
Masking tape

7 Now remove just the split-woven end from the loom, and carefully unwrap the weaving until you reach the end, which has the ten rows of un-split weaving. Carefully twist the split weaving around itself until you have worked the full length.

8 Now wind the roller so the weaving is wound around it again.

9 Wrap a small piece of masking tape around the beads thus holding the twisted weaving in place.

10 Place the knotted warp thread back onto the roller and weave ten rows of basic weaving using both colours **A** and **B**, as you did for the first ten rows.

11 Finish off both ends and attach the glasses holder ends to complete, using Method Three (see page 16).

With the glasses end-caps in place, the cord is complete

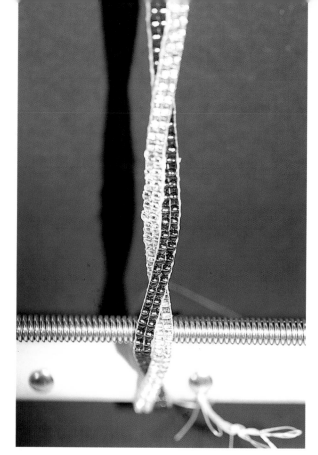

Split weaving section wound around itself

Masking tape placed around weaving to hold it in place

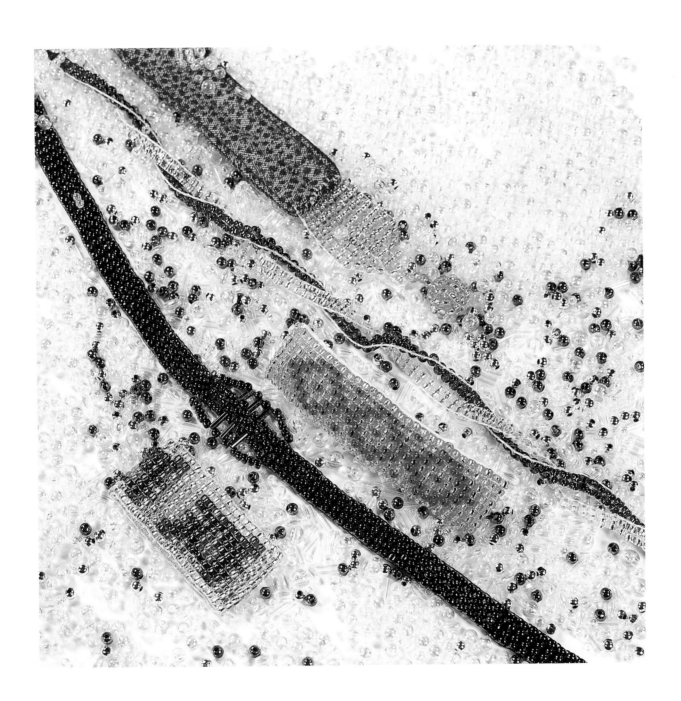

HOME

We all like to add an individual touch
to our homes and to make our mark
on our daily surroundings.
The following projects, which provide
inspiration and patterns for a variety
of items around the home, will allow
you to do just that. So get creating,
and show off your beading talent
to your family and friends.

NAPKIN RINGS

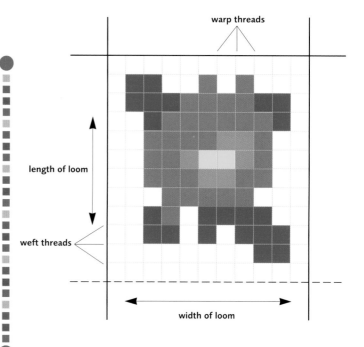

I f you like to show off your best china when entertaining, these beaded napkins rings will complement it beautifully. The first version, Flower Power, is based upon the primrose, but the colourway can be altered to suit your own decor.

VERSION ONE: FLOWER POWER

METHOD

1 Cut 14 pieces of bead thread, each 35cm (14in) long.

2 Thread up the loom, placing double threads on the two outer edges.

MATERIALS

Version One: Flower Power

For one napkin ring you will need basic materials (see page 6) plus

Silver-lined beads (size 11/0) as follows:
102 x purple
18 x orange
6 x yellow
57 x green
213 x clear

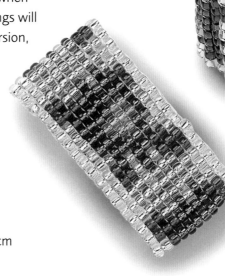

warp threads

length of loom

weft threads

width of loom

Bead-weaving pattern

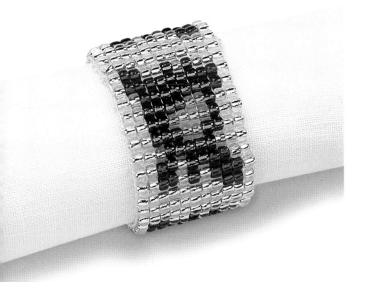

MATERIALS

Version Two: Hot Red

You will need basic materials (see page 6) plus

Silver-lined, red seed beads x 380

3 Following the pattern on the facing page, weave the first flower.

4 Repeat this process twice more to create a napkin ring with three flowers.

5 Remove the finished beading from the loom.

6 To create the ring, bring the weaving around upon itself and tie each corresponding thread to its counterpart on the other end.

7 Once each thread has been tied off, complete the napkin ring by weaving the loose threads through the beading.

VERSION TWO: HOT RED

METHOD

1 Cut 11 threads 35cm (14in) long.

2 Thread up the loom, placing double threads on the two outer edges.

3 Place ten beads on your needle and pass the needle under the threads in the usual manner.

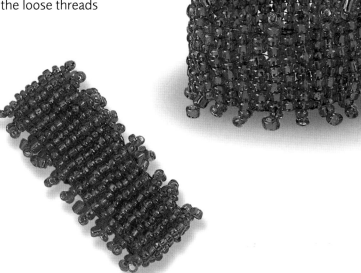

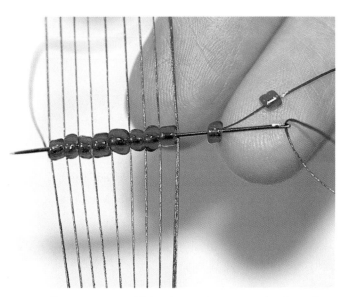

First row woven with bead ten acting as an anchor (step 4)

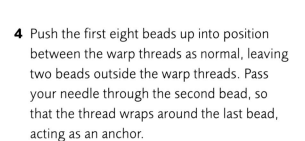

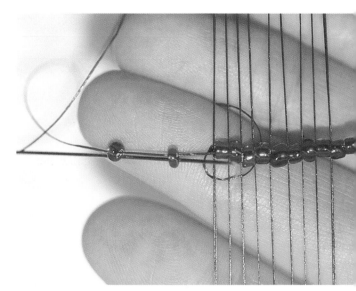

Adding two extra beads onto row at other end and anchoring into place (step 6)

4 Push the first eight beads up into position between the warp threads as normal, leaving two beads outside the warp threads. Pass your needle through the second bead, so that the thread wraps around the last bead, acting as an anchor.

5 Now pass the needle through the beads as normal across the top of the warp thread and through all the beads held between those warp threads.

6 Thread two beads on the weft thread and go back through the bead nearest the warp threads, again allowing the outer bead to act as an anchor.

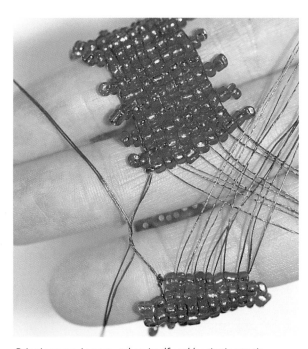

Bringing weaving around on itself and beginning to tie threads (step 11)

7 Wrap the weft thread around the outer two warp threads and pull tightly.

8 Weave the next row as per normal.

9 Weave the third row, following instructions for steps 4 to 7.

10 Repeat this process until you have woven 38 rows.

11 Release the weaving from the loom and curl the weaving around upon itself.

12 Knot each corresponding thread and weave back through the beads to secure.

13 Cut all loose ends.

By altering the number of columns or rows, this pattern can easily be adjusted to make an attractive ring or a bright, eye-catching bracelet.

Knotting corresponding threads (step 12)

TIPS

To strengthen the finished napkin ring, line it with bias binding. To do this, purchase bias binding the same width as your napkin ring. Cut a piece of binding slightly longer than your napkin ring and fold it into a tube so that it is now the same internal size. Sew the two ends together, then place the binding inside the ring and attach with small, neat hand stitching, using the outer thread of the weaving as the anchor for your stitching.

When knotting off, you may find it easier to weave each loose thread through the woven section as you work from one side to the next, and cut the thread as you go. In this way you reduce the number of threads you are working with and it is easier to keep track of each one.

LADYBIRD TRINKET BOX

The small tester pots of paint available from most DIY stores are ideal for decorating this little trinket box and, if you do not have a natural sponge, the design works equally well with a ragged or a washed effect.

METHOD FOR WEAVING THE LADYBIRD

1 Cut 19 pieces of thread 35cm (14in) long and thread the loom with these in the normal way except that, on this occasion, you do not need to double-thread the two outer edges.

2 Weave the ladybird decoration, following the pattern provided.

MATERIALS

You will need basic materials (see page 6) plus

Papier mâché box, sample here measures
7 x 7 x 4cm (2³/₄ x 2³/₄ x 1¹/₂in)
White paint
Dark green paint
Natural sponge
¹/₂in household paint brush
Seed beads (size 11/0) in the following colours:
Light green x 98
Dark green x 119
Black x 38
Red x 132
Double-sided sticky tape

NOTE

The pattern (on the facing page) is a different shape from the beading in the photograph, because I have allowed for the shape of the beads. When completed, the beading will be square, as in the photograph. If you prefer to use Delicas beads, the beading will end up the same shape as this pattern.

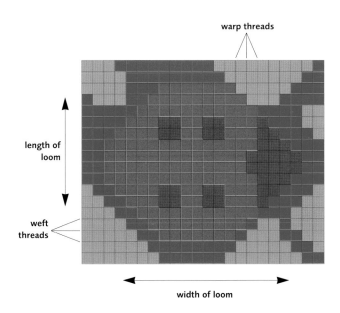

Bead-weaving pattern

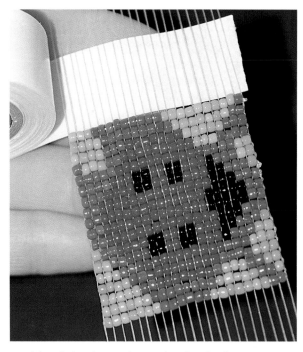

Double-sided sticky tape being placed under the warp threads (step 3)

3 Once woven, complete using Method One (see page 15) for casting off.

4 Next, completely cover the back of the weaving with double-sided sticky tape. It is then ready to be stuck centrally on the trinket box lid. First, though, the box must be decorated, following the instructions overleaf.

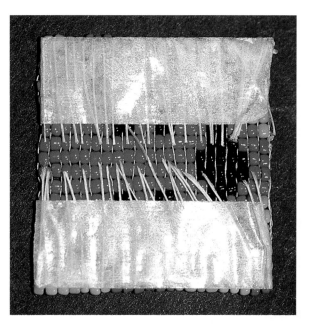

The back of the ladybird, with two pieces of double-sided sticky tape holding the warp threads in place

The middle of the weaving, covered with double-sided sticky tape (step 4)

Box with first coat of white paint (step 1)

METHOD FOR DECORATING THE BOX

1 Separate the lid from the base and coat all the outside edges of the box with the white paint. Allow to dry completely.

2 Once the first coat has dried, sponge on the dark green paint in a random fashion and allow to dry.

3 Once both coats of paint are dry, stick the large woven ladybird in position, centrally on the lid.

Box sponged with dark green paint (step 2)

TIP

If you wish to finish off the box in style, paint the interior as well as the exterior, or you could even line the box with red felt. In addition, you can improve the durability of the paint on the box by applying a coat of clear non-yellowing varnish prior to attaching the beaded ladybird design.

Ladybird in position on the top of the box (step 3)

GREETINGS CARDS

Every year we spend vast sums of money on cards of all shapes and sizes for all manner of occasions. A handmade card, however, is fun and quick to make, is sure to be appreciated, and will show how much you really care.

Here are some suggestions for presenting your weaving in card form. Once you get going you will be able to adapt these designs and come up with a range of your own, showing your own taste in both design and colour.

Mulberry paper, which I've used for the first two cards, is a handmade paper which is available from most good hobby or craft shops.

'Peel 'n' sticks', which I recommend for the greetings on your cards, are foil stickers on a backing sheet, which are peeled off and stuck in position. They are readily available in a wide variety of colours.

Some of the equipment and materials used for card making, including decorative scissors, ribbler (a tool for crinkling card) and craft card

CHRISTMAS TREE CARD

METHOD

1 Weave the Christmas tree following the pattern below. Cast off the weaving using Method One (see page 15) and double-sided sticky tape.

2 Using the decorative scissors, cut the outer edge of the gold card, and stick it centrally on the green card using dry glue stick or double-sided sticky tape.

3 Using a dampened brush, 'draw' a rectangle 8 x 6cm (3 x 2½in) on the mulberry paper, then tear the rectangle out along this dampened line.

MATERIALS

You will need basic materials (see page 6) plus

Seed beads (size 11/0) in the following colours:
Clear x 72
Green x 25
Yellow x 1
Pre-folded green card 10 x 15cm (4 x 6in)
Gold card 9 x 10cm (3½ x 4in)
Mulberry paper 8 x 6cm (3 x 2½in)
Small artist's brush
Pot for water
Dry glue stick or double-side sticky tape
Decorative scissors
Christmas greeting peel 'n' sticks

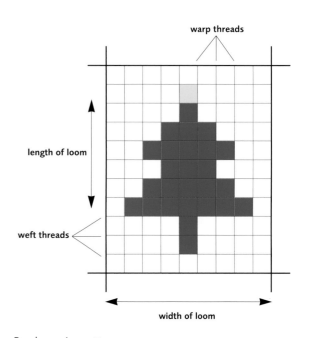

Bead-weaving pattern

Placing the torn mulberry paper on the gold card (step 4)

4 Mount the torn mulberry paper shape centrally on the gold card, allowing space at the top for your chosen greeting.

5 To complete the card, attach the woven Christmas tree with the double-sided sticky tape that you used to cast off, and add your greeting.

Reverse side of the Christmas tree motif, showing the double-sided sticky tape ready for placing centrally on the card (step 5)

REINDEER CHRISTMAS CARD

METHOD

1 Weave the reindeer, following the pattern below, and cast off using Method One (see page 15) and double-sided sticky tape.

2 Fold the piece of A5 card in half across the shorter of the two ends, to make a tall, vertical card with a left-hand fold.

MATERIALS

You will need basic materials (see page 6) plus

Seed beads (size 11/0) in the following colours:
Red x 1
Brown x 4
Yellow x 40
White x 14
Green x 66
A5 card suitable for card backing
Mulberry paper
Double-sided sticky tape or dry glue stick
Fine artists' brush
Pot full of water
Christmas greeting peel 'n' sticks

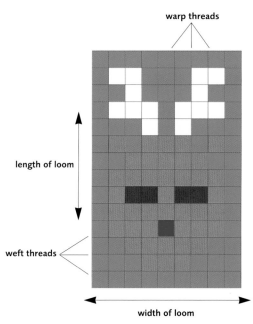

Bead-weaving pattern

3 Using the brush and a little water, 'draw'
out a rectangle on the mulberry paper –
approximately 6 x 11cm (2¼ x 4¼in) – or
a size that will sit comfortably on your card.
Tear the shape out along this damp line.

4 Mount the mulberry paper as shown in the
photograph on the facing page, allowing
room for your Christmas greeting.

5 Fix your chosen peel 'n' stick greeting in place.

6 To complete the card, remove the backing
from the double-sided sticky tape behind the
reindeer motif, and fix in position, centrally on
the mulberry paper.

The mulberry paper torn to size using the water method (step 3)

BIRTHDAY CANDLE CARD

METHOD

1 Weave the candle design following the pattern below, then cast off using Method One (see page 15) and double-sided sticky tape.

2 Fold the card in half along the two longer edges, to make a horizontal card.

MATERIALS

You will need basic materials (see page 6) plus

Seed beads (size 11/0) in the following colours:
Green x 64
White x 44
Yellow x 10
Orange x 6
Red x 2
A5 card suitable for card backing
Small piece of gold card, 4 x 6cm (1½ x 2¼in)
Ribbler
Double-sided sticky tape
Decorative scissors
'Happy Birthday' peel 'n' sticks

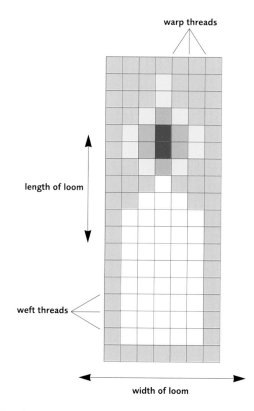

Bead-weaving pattern

3 Cut the piece of gold card 4 x 6cm (1½ x 2¼in) and put through a ribbler to create a textured effect.

4 Position the gold card as shown in the photograph, allowing space for your greeting.

5 Remove the backing from the double-sided sticky tape on the woven design and fold to the back. Mount the candle design on the piece of gold card, as shown.

6 To complete the card, add the peel 'n' stick 'Happy Birthday' greeting.

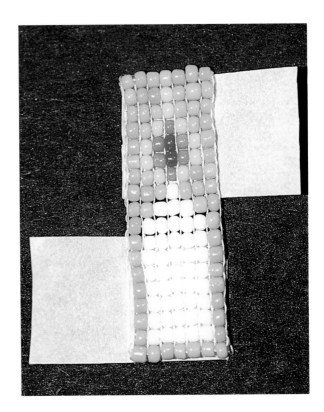

The candle motif cast off using Method One (step 1)

The completed card, ready for the greeting to be added

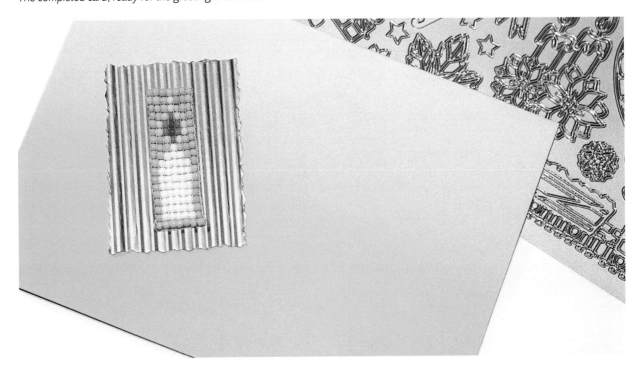

VALENTINE'S DAY CARD

METHOD

1 Weave the heart motif following the pattern and cast off using Method One (see page 15) and double-sided sticky tape.

2 Fold the piece of card in half and, using the decorative scissors, cut to a size of 10 x 10cm (4 x 4in) when folded.

MATERIALS

You will need basic materials (see page 6) plus

Seed beads (size 11/0) in the following colours:
Red x 33
White x 48
A5 red card, suitable for card backing
Piece of silver craft mesh, 5 x 5cm (2 x 2in)
Peel 'n' stick silver 'chain'
Decorative scissors
Pencil
Rule
Scissors
Hot-glue gun or good all-purpose glue
Rubber

The materials for the card

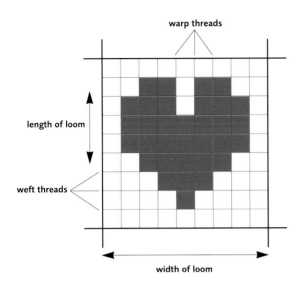

warp threads

length of loom

weft threads

width of loom

Bead-weaving pattern

3 Measure 1.5cm ($^5/_8$in) in from the outer edge all round the card, mark lightly with a pencil, then draw a faint line in all round.

4 Using the pencilled line as your guide, stick the 'chain' in place.

5 Cut the wire mesh to the size stated above, then mount it centrally on the card, by placing a blob of all-purpose glue in the centre only. (This is to ensure that the glue won't show once the heart motif is in position.)

6 To complete the card, turn the double-sided sticky tape to the reverse of your woven design and stick the woven heart in the centre of the craft mesh.

Outer decoration being placed onto the card following pencil marking (step 4)

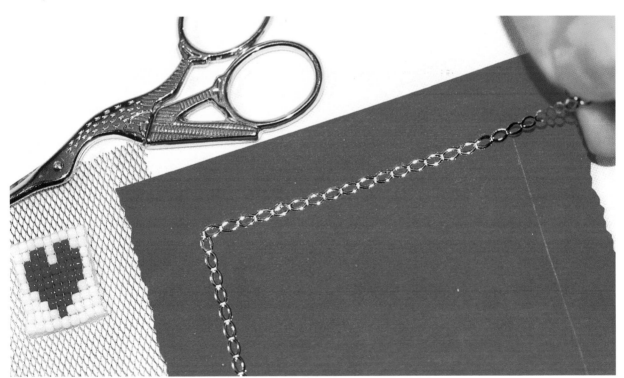

LADYBIRD CARD

METHOD

1 Weave the ladybird following the pattern below, then cast off using Method Two (see page 16).

2 Trace the flower template onto the watercolour paper, then cut out the shape.

3 Colour the flower using the water-soluble pencils, then pick out the details as shown, using the fine-line black pen.

4 Fold the piece of card in half, then mount the flower on the card a few millimetres (¹/₈in) in from the folded edge.

MATERIALS

You will need basic materials (see page 6) plus

Seed beads (size 11/0) in the following colours:
Black x 8
Red x 26
A5 craft card suitable for card backing
A6 watercolour paper
Orange and red water-soluble pencils
Fine artist's brush
Pot of water
Pencil
Eraser
Scissors
Fine-line black pen
Hot-glue gun or good all-purpose glue (clear drying)
Dry glue stick

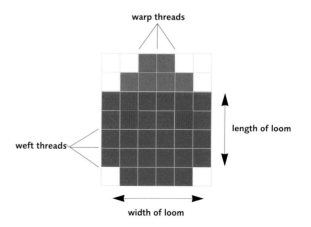

Bead-weaving pattern

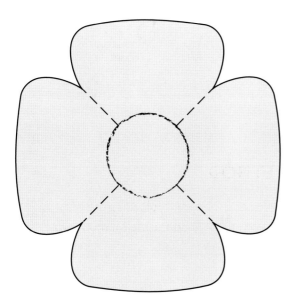

Card pattern. Enlarge by 140% to use as template

Ladybird weaving cast off and ready to be mounted onto card

5 Cut around the outer edge, leaving a small border around the flower, but be careful not to cut the folded edge.

6 To complete the card, stick the ladybird in position using the hot-glue gun or all-purpose glue.

Flower coloured using water soluble pencils (step 3)

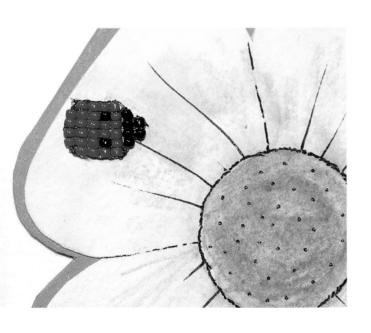

Card complete with ladybird stuck into position

NOTE

The designs shown here are not the only ones that could be used for cards. Have a look at the patterns with the other projects, and see if you can tailor-make a special one.

A FEW MORE BEAD-WEAVING PATTERNS FOR CARDS, TO GIVE YOU INSPIRATION

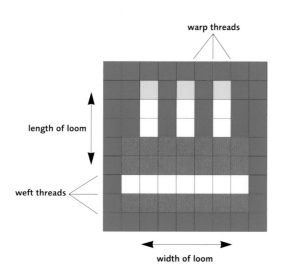

Alternative birthday card

'New home' card

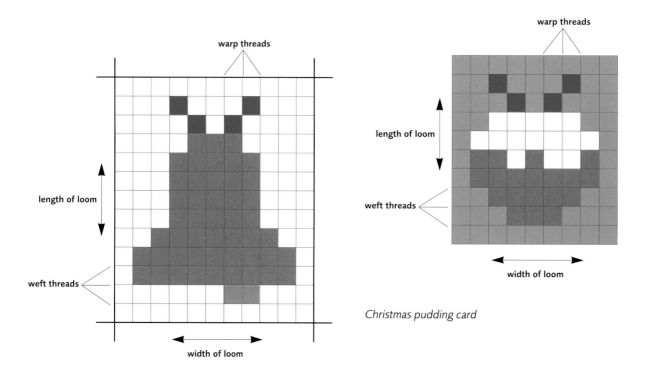

Christmas bell card

Christmas pudding card

PICTURE FRAME

We all love to show off favourite images of our family and pets but sometimes it is difficult to find the right frame to match the image. This tiger-striped frame will, hopefully, solve that problem. If you like, you can substitute white beads for the yellow, to make a zebra-striped frame.

This pattern could also be used to transform a small bedside mirror. So two looks for the price of one!

MATERIALS

You will need basic materials (see page 6) plus

Clip frame, 10 x 15cm (4 x 6in)
Seed beads (size 11/0) in the following colours:
Yellow x 854 (or white, for zebra stripes)
Black x 764
Double-sided sticky tape or good all-purpose clear-drying glue
A5 white or yellow card
Pencil
Steel rule
Craft knife

NOTE:

The beading patterns overleaf are not drawn according to scale of bead size being used but, provided you use the recommended size of beads, then the pattern should produce a piece of weaving which fits the frame suggested. To ensure that your weaving does fit the frame, measure on a regular basis, as any difference in bead size will obviously affect the size of the finished weaving.

warp threads

length of loom

weft threads

width of loom

Bead-weaving pattern for left and right sides

METHOD

1 Following the pattern, weave the two sides and finish off using Method One (see page 15).

2 Now place these to one side while you weave the top and bottom sections.

TIP

If the frame is to be used in a bathroom, or a room where it may get damp, fix the bead work in place with multi-purpose clear-drying glue rather than sticky tape, as it will hold better.

Warp threads of the top section threaded through the side section (step 3)

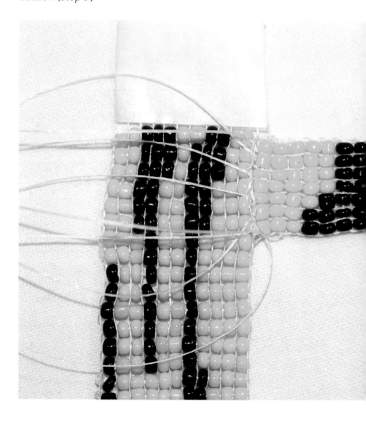

3 When complete, don't knot the ends, as these threads are used to attach the top and bottom weaving to the two side panels; to do this, tie the warp threads of the top and bottom sections to the outer warp threads of the two side panels.

4 Once all the ends are tied off, cover the back of the weaving with double-sided sticky tape.

NOTE

Methylated spirits, white spirits, or nail varnish remover are all good for removing dirty marks from the glass, but make sure they have evaporated completely prior to sticking the beadwork into place.

All threads knotted and cut (step 3)

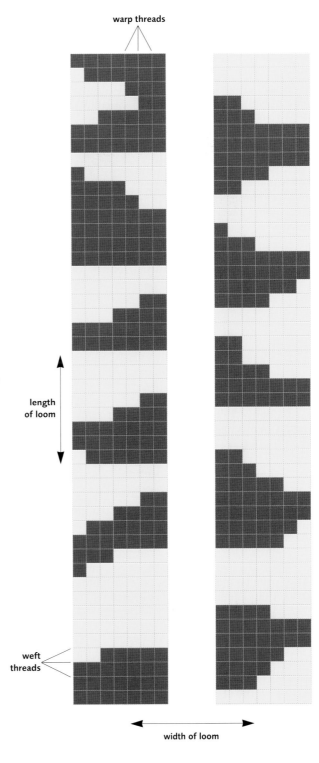

Bead-weaving patterns (above):
Bottom of frame (left)   *Top of frame (right)*

The reverse of the beadwork, covered with double-sided sticky tape (step 5)

5 Remove the backing from the tape and place the woven section face down.

6 Take the frame apart and clean the glass to make sure that any dirt and grease are removed.

7 Now bring the glass down into contact with the beading and, checking first that the sides match up, gently push down with the tips of your fingers (do not use too much pressure) until the tape and beadwork come into contact with the glass.

8 Prior to fixing your image in the frame, cut a mount out of the white or yellow card. Mark out an aperture that matches the aperture created by the beadwork and carefully cut out using the craft knife and steel rule.

9 Once cut, mount your picture and position in pride of place.

If you would like to add further decorative detail to the finished item, create a looped fringe inside the aperture using either the yellow or the black beads (see instructions for loop fringing on page 19).

BOOKMARK

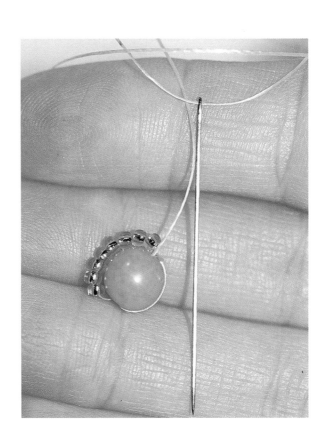

There is nothing worse than returning to a book and finding that you have lost your place. This attractive bookmark resolves that problem and would be the ideal gift for an avid reader.

METHOD FOR CREATING YOUR OWN ACCENT BEAD

1 Thread your needle with a piece of thread approximately 40cm (16in) long and pass through the middle hole of the large round bead.

2 Tie off this thread using a double knot around the large bead.

Starting to create the accent bead (step 4)

MATERIALS

You will need basic materials (see page 6) plus

Seed beads (size 11/0) x 130 (including those for customizing the large bead)
Large round bead, approximately 1cm (³/₈in), in complementary colour to seed beads
Lightweight fabric, 2 pieces, each 5 x 26cm (2 x 10¹/₂in)
Sewing thread to match the fabric
Sewing machine (not essential, but recommended)

The accent bead covered with a couple lines of beads (step 5)

The completed accent bead (step 6)

3 Now place a number of seed beads onto the thread, so that the total length reached spans from the top to the bottom of the large bead.

4 When you have enough beads on your thread, pass the needle through the hole and pull the thread tight.

5 Repeat until the large bead is covered with smaller beads. N.B. Near the end of this process you may find that you need to reduce the number of beads on your thread for each span.

6 When the bead is covered, do not cut the remaining length of thread, as it is used to attach the bead to your weaving a little later.

METHOD FOR WEAVING THE DESIGN

1 Set your loom up with 13 threads, each at least 44cm (17in) long, and place two threads on the outer edges for added strength.

2 Weaving ten beads per row, create seven rows of weaving.

3 On the eighth row weave using just eight beads, missing off a bead at both ends.

4 Repeat this process, decreasing one bead at each end until you reach a row containing just two beads.

The completed piece of weaving with the accent bead attached to the pointed end (step 2 overleaf)

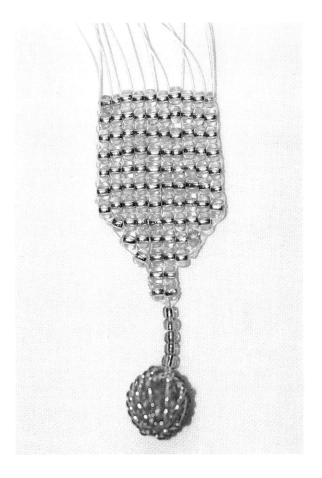

5 Casting off: at this time do not cast off the fatter end of your weaving as these threads will be used to attach the weaving to the main body of the bookmark. Use Method Two for casting off the other end (see page 16), but do not cut off the last three threads here, either, as they will be used to attach the large accent bead.

METHOD FOR SEWING THE MAIN BODY OF BOOKMARK

1 Cut out the fabric to the size specified.

2 Place right sides and together sew around three of the edges (leaving one of the shortest edges open) using a 1cm (³/₈in) seam allowance.

3 Turn inside out, so the right sides are on top, then press.

4 Turn in the top open edge and sew a line of stitching around the outer edge of the whole bookmark, to give a neat finish.

TO ASSEMBLE THE BOOKMARK

1 Take the accent bead and place four beads onto the thread left uncut in step 6 of 'Method for creating your own accent bead'.

Main body of bookmark complete with outer decorative sewing line (step 4, above)

2 Attach this bead to the woven section on the end that has been decreased to just the two beads, using the threads left from the casting-off process. Weave all these threads back into the beading and cut off any loose ends.

3 Attach the weaving to one end of the bookmark, by threading the uncut loose threads from casting off onto a needle one thread at a time, then securing well with a knot. Pass the loose end down the inside body of the bookmark. Bring the needle out and cut off the loose end close to the bookmark.

4 Continue until all the threads have been dealt with in this manner. Your bookmark is then complete.

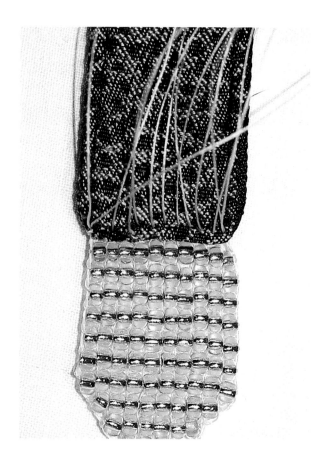

Attaching the woven section of the bookmark to the sewn fabric section (step 3)

WHERE TO OBTAIN FURTHER INSPIRATION

Although this book contains a variety of beading patterns, which can be adjusted to suit your own needs and tastes, there are many other sources available to you. For instance, if you find a cross-stitch pattern that you like, it can easily be adapted to suit a bead-weaving item. Bear in mind, however, that with cross stitch the stitches are completely square, while seed beads are a little uneven in shape (being wider than they are long) and this will affect the overall shape of your finished item. As mentioned before, this problem can be overcome with the use of Delicas beads, which are as long as they are wide, but remember that, if you use them for the projects in this book, they will change the size of the finished weaving.

There are also books that cover the great crafts of counted beadwork, plastic canvaswork and knitting. Again the patterns in these books are ideal for bead weaving. And lastly, if you see a design you like that is not already in pattern form, you can convert it to a pattern which will enable you to create your own individual bead-woven piece. There are books on the market which teach you to do just this and, in today's computer-driven age, there are even software packages which will help you to create your own patterns.

BIBLIOGRAPHY AND FURTHER READING

During the research for this book I read many books and below are the titles which I found exceptionally informative, inspiring and fun to read. So, if you truly get the bug for weaving, it would be worth taking a trip to your library to see if you can track down any of the following books.

Stanley-Miller, Pamela
Authentic American Indian Beadwork and How To Do It
Dover Publications Inc.
ISBN 0 486 24739 2

Thompson, Angela
Embroidery with Beads
B.T. Batsford Ltd
ISBN 0 7134 5495 4

Ketchum Jr, William C.
Native American Art
Todtri Productions Ltd
ISBN 1 85501 942 6

Taylor Ph.D., Colin F. (Editorial Consultant)
Native American Arts and Crafts
Salamander Books Ltd
ISBN 0 86101 786 2

Jones, Julia
The Beading Book
A. & C. Black Ltd
ISBN 0 7136 3787 0

Donald, Elsie Buron
The Book of Creative Crafts
Book Club Associates
ISBN 0 7064 0883 7

Books are not the only source of good information on this wonderful craft; we now have the Internet, which is evolving all the time. Type in Native American bead weaving on any of the search engines and you will be astounded by the wealth of information on offer. During my research for this book these are just a few of the websites I found.

http://suzannecooper.com/classroom/loom/html

http://www.si.edu/resource/faq.nacrafts.htm

http://www.nativetech.org

This is obviously just the tip of the iceberg. I am sure you will find further useful resources which were not available to me during the writing of this book.

Suppliers of General Crafts

United Kingdom

Fred Aldous
PO Box 135
37 Lever Street
Manchester
M1 1LW
Enquiries: 0161 236 2477
Orders: 0161 236 4224
Craft/hobby suppliers from own shop or via post

Rocking Rabbit
226A High Street
Cottenham
Cambridge
CB4 8RZ
Tel: 0870 606 1588
Email: sales@rockingrabbit.co.uk
Bead and craft suppliers via mail

Panduro Hobby
Westway House
Transport Avenue
Brentford
Middlesex
TW8 9HF
Customer Services: 020 8847 6161
Website: www.panduro.co.uk
Craft and bead suppliers by post

Plaid UK Ltd
Mill Lane
Greenhill Lane
Ridding
Derbyshire
DE55 4EX
Tel: 01773 540808
Craft/hobby suppliers

Craft Creations
Ingersoll House
Delamare Road
Cheshunt,
Herts
EN8 9HD
Tel: 01992 781900
Website: www.craftcreations.com
Craft and card-making suppliers, from shop or by post

USA

Darice
Main Office
13000 Darice Parkway
Park 82
Strongsville
Ohio 44136 6699
USA
Website: www.darice.com
Supplier of craft materials

ABOUT THE AUTHOR

For the past six years Lynne Garner has worked at local colleges teaching a variety of crafts, including glass painting, pottery, sewing, interior design and papercrafts. She also teaches environmental studies to teenagers with special needs.

Lynne has contributed articles to many magazines, including *Creative Crafts for the Home*, *Making Cards*, *Yours*, *Stamping Arts and Crafts* and *RubberStampMadness* and she has been writing regular rubber stamping and review columns for *Popular Crafts* magazine since July 1997.

In her spare time Lynne enjoys wildlife watching, as well as looking after sick, injured and orphaned hedgehogs in the 'hedgehog hospital' she has made in her converted garage. Once the hedegehogs have recovered, she releases them back into the wild.

She loves to take wildlife photographs and is a member of The Society of Authors and the Nature Photography Association.

Further examples of Lynne's work can be viewed on her website: www.lynnegarner.com

INDEX

TITLES AVAILABLE FROM
GMC Publications

BOOKS

WOODCARVING

Beginning Woodcarving	GMC Publications
Carving Architectural Detail in Wood: The Classical Tradition	Frederick Wilbur
Carving Birds & Beasts	GMC Publications
Carving the Human Figure: Studies in Wood and Stone	Dick Onians
Carving Nature: Wildlife Studies in Wood	Frank Fox-Wilson
Celtic Carved Lovespoons: 30 Patterns	Sharon Littley & Clive Griffin
Decorative Woodcarving (New Edition)	Jeremy Williams
Elements of Woodcarving	Chris Pye
Figure Carving in Wood: Human and Animal Forms	Sara Wilkinson
Lettercarving in Wood: A Practical Course	Chris Pye
Relief Carving in Wood: A Practical Introduction	Chris Pye
Woodcarving for Beginners	GMC Publications
Woodcarving Made Easy	Cynthia Rogers
Woodcarving Tools, Materials & Equipment (New Edition in 2 vols.)	Chris Pye

WOODTURNING

Bowl Turning Techniques Masterclass	Tony Boase
Chris Child's Projects for Woodturners	Chris Child
Decorating Turned Wood: The Maker's Eye	Liz & Michael O'Donnell
Green Woodwork	Mike Abbott
Keith Rowley's Woodturning Projects	Keith Rowley
Making Screw Threads in Wood	Fred Holder
Segmented Turning: A Complete Guide	Ron Hampton
Turned Boxes: 50 Designs	Chris Stott
Turning Green Wood	Michael O'Donnell
Turning Pens and Pencils	Kip Christensen & Rex Burningham
Woodturning: Forms and Materials	John Hunnex
Woodturning: A Foundation Course (New Edition)	Keith Rowley
Woodturning: A Fresh Approach	Robert Chapman
Woodturning: An Individual Approach	Dave Regester
Woodturning: A Source Book of Shapes	John Hunnex
Woodturning Masterclass	Tony Boase

WOODWORKING

Beginning Picture Marquetry	Lawrence Threadgold
Celtic Carved Lovespoons: 30 Patterns	Sharon Littley & Clive Griffin
Celtic Woodcraft	Glenda Bennett
Complete Woodfinishing (Revised Edition)	Ian Hosker
David Charlesworth's Furniture-Making Techniques	David Charlesworth
David Charlesworth's Furniture-Making Techniques – Volume 2	David Charlesworth
Furniture Projects with the Router	Kevin Ley
Furniture Restoration (Practical Crafts)	Kevin Jan Bonner
Furniture Restoration: A Professional at Work	John Lloyd
Green Woodwork	Mike Abbott
Intarsia: 30 Patterns for the Scrollsaw	John Everett
Making Heirloom Boxes	Peter Lloyd
Making Screw Threads in Wood	Fred Holder
Making Woodwork Aids and Devices	Robert Wearing
Mastering the Router	Ron Fox
Pine Furniture Projects for the Home	Dave Mackenzie

Router Magic: Jigs, Fixtures and Tricks to Unleash your Router's Full Potential	Bill Hylton
Router Projects for the Home	GMC Publications
Router Tips & Techniques	Robert Wearing
Routing: A Workshop Handbook	Anthony Bailey
Routing for Beginners	Anthony Bailey
Stickmaking: A Complete Course	Andrew Jones & Clive George
Stickmaking Handbook	Andrew Jones & Clive George
Storage Projects for the Router	GMC Publications
Veneering: A Complete Course	Ian Hosker
Veneering Handbook	Ian Hosker
Woodworking Techniques and Projects	Anthony Bailey
Woodworking with the Router: Professional Router Techniques any Woodworker can Use	Bill Hylton & Fred Matlack

UPHOLSTERY

Upholstery: A Complete Course (Revised Edition)	David James
Upholstery Restoration	David James
Upholstery Techniques & Projects	David James
Upholstery Tips and Hints	David James

DOLLS' HOUSES AND MINIATURES

1/12 Scale Character Figures for the Dolls' House	James Carrington
Americana in 1/12 Scale: 50 Authentic Projects	Joanne Ogreenc & Mary Lou Santovec
The Authentic Georgian Dolls' House	Brian Long
A Beginners' Guide to the Dolls' House Hobby	Jean Nisbett
Celtic, Medieval and Tudor Wall Hangings in 1/12 Scale Needlepoint	Sandra Whitehead
Creating Decorative Fabrics: Projects in 1/12 Scale	Janet Storey
Dolls' House Accessories, Fixtures and Fittings	Andrea Barham
Dolls' House Furniture: Easy-to-Make Projects in 1/12 Scale	Freida Gray
Dolls' House Makeovers	Jean Nisbett
Dolls' House Window Treatments	Eve Harwood
Edwardian-Style Hand-Knitted Fashion for 1/12 Scale Dolls	Yvonne Wakefield
How to Make Your Dolls' House Special: Fresh Ideas for Decorating	Beryl Armstrong
Making 1/12 Scale Wicker Furniture for the Dolls' House	Sheila Smith
Making Miniature Chinese Rugs and Carpets	Carol Phillipson
Making Miniature Food and Market Stalls	Angie Scarr
Making Miniature Gardens	Freida Gray
Making Miniature Oriental Rugs & Carpets	Meik & Ian McNaughton
Making Miniatures: Projects for the 1/12 Scale Dolls' House	Christiane Berridge
Making Period Dolls' House Accessories	Andrea Barham
Making Tudor Dolls' Houses	Derek Rowbottom
Making Upholstered Furniture in 1/12 Scale	Janet Storey
Medieval and Tudor Needlecraft: Knights and Ladies in 1/12 Scale	Sandra Whitehead
Miniature Bobbin Lace	Roz Snowden
Miniature Crochet: Projects in 1/12 Scale	Roz Walters
Miniature Embroidery for the Georgian Dolls' House	Pamela Warner

VIDEOS

Drop-in and Pinstuffed Seats	*David James*	Twists and Advanced Turning	*Dennis White*
Stuffover Upholstery	*David James*	Sharpening the Professional Way	*Jim Kingshott*
Elliptical Turning	*David Springett*	Sharpening Turning & Carving Tools	*Jim Kingshott*
Woodturning Wizardry	*David Springett*	Bowl Turning	*John Jordan*
Turning Between Centres: The Basics	*Dennis White*	Hollow Turning	*John Jordan*
Turning Bowls	*Dennis White*	Woodturning: A Foundation Course	*Keith Rowley*
Boxes, Goblets and Screw Threads	*Dennis White*	Carving a Figure: The Female Form	*Ray Gonzalez*
Novelties and Projects	*Dennis White*	The Router: A Beginner's Guide	*Alan Goodsell*
Classic Profiles	*Dennis White*	The Scroll Saw: A Beginner's Guide	*John Burke*

MAGAZINES

WOODTURNING ◆ WOODCARVING ◆ FURNITURE & CABINETMAKING

THE ROUTER ◆ NEW WOODWORKING ◆ THE DOLLS' HOUSE MAGAZINE

OUTDOOR PHOTOGRAPHY ◆ BLACK & WHITE PHOTOGRAPHY

MACHINE KNITTING NEWS ◆ KNITTING

GUILD OF MASTER CRAFTSMEN NEWS

The above represents a full list of all titles currently published or scheduled to be published.
All are available direct from the Publishers or through bookshops, newsagents and specialist retailers.
To place an order, or to obtain a complete catalogue, contact:

GMC Publications,
Castle Place, 166 High Street, Lewes, East Sussex BN7 1XU United Kingdom
Tel: 01273 488005 Fax: 01273 478606
E-mail: pubs@thegmcgroup.com

Orders by credit card are accepted